CHOCOLATE DROPS

From the South

A Book of Negro Humor and Philosophy

by

E. V. WHITE

THE E. L. STECK COMPANY, Publishers

Austin

Printed in the U. S. A.

PREFACE

The American Negro has been our Nation's greatest source of genuine laughter and good humor. He looks funny, he acts funny, he is funny. Moreover, he is serious about it all. Without this genial contribution, America would not be America.

This little book is a collection of Negro stories that have been and are the common property of our country. No person has a right to claim them — they belong to every one. Hence, no claim of originality is made for their content. But the setting, the peculiar psychology, and the natural dialect contain certain points of originality that emanate from a life of contact with the Negro race.

For the most part, only the stories that are true to the psychology of the Negro race have been included in the collection. They touch the subjects of war and religion, love and hate, courtship and marriage, death and divorce, courts and combats, food and foolishness, diplomacy and philosophy. The superiority of Negro stories lies in the fact that they include such a wide range of the human emotions. Most of the group have been published previously by piecemeal, but many of them are told for the first time in printed form.

It is believed that the professional man, the club member, the lecturer, the student, the fun-maker, and most important of all — the lover of good-natured humor, will appreciate these stories about a people who are happy and hopeful, helpful and harmless, despite the injustices so often imposed upon them.

E. V. WHITE.

CLASSIFICATION OF CONTENTS

CLASSIFICATION OF CONTENTS
Continued

CALL THE SHERIFF

Jake and Mose, always broke, were overheard discussing their financial difficulties, in the following conversation:

Jake: "Mose, 'spose yo' wuz tuh git up in de mawnin', slip on yo' britches, put yo' han's in yo' pocket, an' fin' two hund'ed dollahs."

Mose: "Yeh, but dat ain't gonna happen, 'case Ah's busted an' hit ain't no use thinkin' whut ain't gonna be."

Jake: "Yeh, boy, but 'spose hit did happen, an' yo' run yo' han's down in yo' britches pocket an' fin' two hund'ed dollahs, whut would yo' think, Mose?"

Mose: "Ah'll tell yo' whut Ah'd think. Ah'd jes' think Ah had on de wrong britches."

WORTH THE MONEY

A certain justice of the peace down in Texas was often called upon to perform marriage ceremonies. The official had no uniform price for uniting white people, that being determined by the apparent prosperity of the contracting parties. But for colored people he had a uniform price of two dollars.

A large sinewy looking colored man, accompanied by a young, plump, extremely black damsel, appeared at the office of the justice. After the marriage ceremony, the groom asked the official how much he owed.

"Two dollars," answered the justice of the peace.

"Boss, dat sho' does look mouty steep fuh jes' fo' minits ob yo' time," said the Negro. "Ah wuhks hahd all day fuh two dollahs."

"Yes, but that kiss you gave the bride while ago was worth two dollars."

"Well, boss," answered the darkey mournfully, "jes' he'p yo' se'f!"

AN INDEFINITE ANSWER

A group of men, on a hunting expedition, had established their camp at a convenient place near the river. They were fortunate in procuring a Negro man, who lived within a short distance, to prepare food regularly for the party. Sam was not only proficient in the art of good cooking, but he also contributed to the good feeling of the occasion with a bountiful supply of original wit and genial good humor.

Late in the afternoon, one of the party observed a swarm of pickaninnies in front of the cabin nearby. He asked Sam if all the children were his. The Negro stepped out, looked over the crowd carefully, and ad-

vised that all of them were his own offspring.

"How many children are in the group?"
asked the white man.

"Twelve," answered Sam.

"Do you have any other children?" he
asked.

"Well, suh," replied Sam, with a twinkle
in his eye, "Ah ain't got no mo' on dis side
ob de rivah."

BYE-BYE BLACKBIRD

A dwarfed-sized Negro was on trial in
Arkansas for the murder of Lem Johnson,
another darkey. The case proceeded to the
point where the defendant was testifying
in his own behalf. He admitted that shortly before the tragedy he had approached the
gigantic Lem Johnson from the rear, placed
the muzzle of a double-barreled shot gun to
Lem's back, and pulled the trigger, with a
result that gave him supreme joy.

"Why did you do that?" the prosecuting
attorney asked.

"Well, suh, it wuz lak dis," answered the
runty defendant. "Dat Niggah, Lem, wuz
de meanes' black man Ah evah seen. He wuz
always pickin' on folks, an' de day befo', he
smacked me ovah an' spanked me down. Ah
couldn't whup 'im, he wuz fo' times big as

me, an' Ah didn't have no knife an' no gun. De bes' Ah could do wuz go home, git down by mah baid, an' pray de good Lawd tuh guide me. Yas, suh, dat's whut Ah done. Ah ast Him whut tuh do, an' He tol' me. An' Ah replied back: 'Much obliged, Lawd, Ah's gwine'r sen' yo' a big, black, fightin' scound'el dis very tonight or come mahself'!'"

GONE DEMOCRATIC

Uncle Charley, an humble old darkey who was born in slavery, continued to live near the home of his former master, a distinguished Southern educator. Politically, Charley was a staunch Republican. He earned his living by driving a one-mule express wagon about town.

One day as he drove on the railroad tracks, his mule and wagon were struck by a northbound train, killing the mule, demolishing the wagon, and throwing the old Negro upon the embankment where he was badly stunned. When his former master hurried to the scene of the accident, he found Charley sitting on the ground, with his hands clasped about his knees, in deep meditation.

"Why Charley, what in the world has happened?" exclaimed his white friend.

Scanning his eyes over the wreckage, Charley said very earnestly: "Mistah Randolph, de whole damn thing have done gone Democratic!"

A WISE GENERATION

Uncle Monroe, a white-haired country Negro, visited a city for the first time. Walking through the park, he found $2.85 which enabled him to take his first ride on the street car. To the old darkey, the stopping and calling of the names of streets indicated miraculous power.

"Lawdy," mused Monroe to himself, "dat man is sho' smaht. He calls Washington, an' Mistah Washington git off. Den he calls Adams, an' Mistah Adams git off. Den he calls Jefferson, an' Mistah Jefferson git off. But he doan know mah name an' he cain't put me off." Just then the conductor called "Monroe!".

"Yas, suh, Ah's Monroe. Heah Ah comes." And as he stepped off the car, he marveled at the knowledge of the conductor. Then, a big touring car drove up, and the driver inquired, "Is this Monroe?"

"Yas, suh, dis am Monroe," answered the Negro.

"Good," said the driver, "I'm looking for 285."

"Mah Lawd!" exclaimed the old darkey, reaching for the purse, "dese sho' is awful smaht white folks!"

SIMPLE ADDITION

During the War, a prominent citizen of the South rendered valuable field service in the Fourth Liberty Loan drive. He took upon himself the task of selling to the Negroes of the cotton section of a Southern State. One day his attention was attracted to the genial smile of a middle-aged Negro named Gene.

"Do you know any one in the army?" asked the distinguished citizen.

"Ah suttinly does—mah boys is in de army," answered the darkey.

"How many boys do you have in the army?"

"Fo'teen, suh."

"What? You don't mean to tell me you have fourteen sons!"

"Yas, suh, fo'teen in de army, an' dat ain't all. Ah has three mo' dat will soon be in."

"You mean to tell me you have seventeen sons!"

"Yas, suh, seventeen big boys, an' dat ain't all. Ah has fo' mo' little boys tuh home."

"Twenty-one sons! And only married once! And you still a middle-aged man! I don't understand how this is possible," marveled the visitor.

"Well, suh," said Gene in a confidential tone, "ob dem fo'teen dat am in de army, yo' see dar am fo' pairs ob twins an' two sets of triplets. Dat am fo'teen, ain't hit?"

In the Dark of the Night

Two dusky urchins harbored much contempt for each other. Each hated the way the other looked, talked, or spoke, and the following conversation was typical of their intense hatred:

First Urchin: "Hello dar, Midnight."

Second Urchin: "Huh! Wharfo' yo' speaks tuh me lak dat?"

First Urchin: "Ah say, hello dar, Midnight. Yo' ain't deef. Yo' heah'd me de fus' time."

Second Urchin: "Jus' min' yo' own bizness, Niggah. Yo' needn't be stretchin' yo' neck lak dat, an' lookin' lak dat, an' talkin' lak dat. Yo' looks lak 'bout 'lebben-thirty yo'se'f."

Traveler: "Isn't this air exhilarating?"

Porter: "No, suh, this air Gawgy!"

IDENTIFYING THE DEAD

Ephriam Lamar was a fair average among the Negroes of the community. He had only two faults—he would not work and he occasionally shot craps. Despite these faults, an elaborate funeral was planned when he suddenly passed into the Great Beyond.

The last rites were conducted at the lodge where he had been a faithful attendant for many years. Among the mourners were his widow and a group of pickaninnies ranging from four to sixteen years of age. Great crowds had assembled to pay homage to his memory. One by one, the brothers of the lodge spoke of his high character. They vied with one another in eulogistic extravagances, and the longer the services continued the more complimentary became the exaggerations.

His widow listened intently and bore her bereavement with remarkable equanimity. Finally, when the eulogies reached a climax, she could restrain herself no longer. Leaning over to one of the little pickaninnies, she said:

"Go ovah dar, Lazrus, raise up dat lid, an' see ef dat's yo' Pa whut's in dat coffin."

IGNORANCE IS BLISS

A county Republican convention, consisting largely of Negroes, was in session in a Southern State. The blacks were divided into two very hostile camps, each struggling for supremacy in the distribution of political pie.

A prominent leader in one of the factions was a gaunt Negro, known locally as Goose Neck Bill, who was a good organizer and an orator of no mean ability. He was hated intensely by the opposing faction, and they accredited him with much political trickery.

When the Committee on Nominations made its report, one of the leaders inquired as to the committee assignment of Goose Neck Bill. He was informed that Goose Neck was to be chairman of the Ways and Means Committee.

"Den he sho' am in de right place," retorted the leader. "Dat Niggah knows moah ways ob bein' mean dan any udder cullud puhson in dis whole convention assem'led!"

Big Black: "Does yo' call me a liah, does yo'?"

Little Black: "No suh, sho' not. Ah jes' wishes tuh infer yo' only has elephantiasis ob de 'magination!"

GOOD POLITICS

In his campaign Governor Dan Moody of Texas had made a vigorous attack upon the Ku Klux Klan. A favorite slogan of his supporters was, "Dan's the Man." The morning after the contest closed, when his election was assured, a white man met a colored porter on the train.

"Dan's the Man," said the white.

"He sho' am," said the Negro.

"Let's hear you say it—Dan's the Man."

"Sho' Ah can—Dan's de Man," answered the Negro.

"Now," said the man, "when Dan goes into the Governor's office, and you want to make a call on him, all you will have to do is to go down, knock on the door and say: 'Dan's the Man'. If the door doesn't open, knock again and say: 'Dan's the Man—Damn the Klan.' Come on, let's hear you say it."

"No suh, Boss, Ah kin say de fus' paht all right; but dat las' paht—Ah cain't even whispah dat."

Mistress: "Why do you want your job back, Liza? Married life unhappy? December married to May, perhaps?"

Liza: "It wuz mo' la'k Labor Day married to de Day ob Rest!"

Extra-Legal Relations

Two immaculately groomed and self-confident young men, Sambo and Rufus Rastus, were social lions among the fair sex of their race. They had not seen each other for many months. Then they met, one day, on the street corner, greeting each other cordially, each making diligent inquiry as to the other's welfare. The following conversation ensued:

Rufus Rastus: "Ah's jus' doin' fine. Ah makes fo' dollahs an' six bits a day an' goes tuh de movin' pictur' wid mah gal evah' night. How is yo' gittin' 'long, Sambo?"

Sambo: "Mo' better dan evah. Yo' knows dat Niggah, 'Liza Jane, don't yo'?"

Rufus Rastus: "Co'se Ah knows dat Niggah, 'Liza Jane—we's awful good frien's."

Sambo: "Well me an' her gits married 'bout fo' months ago."

Rufus Rastus: "Yo' did! Yo' don't tell me! Yo' know Ah married dat very same Niggah mahse'f once—we mus' be *husban's-in-law.*"

Sambo: "Heah's dat quarter Ah borrowed frum yo' las' yeah."

Jumbo: "Keep hit, black boy. Tain't wuth while changin' mah 'pinion of yo' jes' fuh two bits!"

In Sacred Memory

A Negro sexton at a cemetery was brought into police court, charged with assault and battery upon a fat Negro woman who was the complaining witness. "Do you state," said the judge, "that this defendant attacked you with malice aforethought and severely beat you?"

"Yas, suh, jedge, Ah suttinly does."

"Then tell your story to the court," said the judge.

"Well, suh, jedge," said the woman, "hit wuz lak dis: Ah wuz gwine th'u de cemetery yestiddy mawnin', tuh do some washin' fuh Miz Brown, an' widout me sayin' a wuhd dis Niggah ups an' says, 'Hello, Sloofoot'; an' Ah says, 'Hello, ole Fish-mouf'. Den he sez, 'Don't yo' gib me none ob yo' sass', an' Ah sez, 'Don't yo' mess wid me, Niggah'. Den, jedge, he ups an' slaps mah face an' slams me jes' as hahd as he could agin a tombstone."

"Are there any marks of violence on your body?" inquired the judge.

"Is dey?" she said. "W'y, jedge, dar is a big place on mah hip, whar dat Niggah slam me agin de tombstone, dat still say, 'Sacred tuh de mem'ry ob somebody'."

Early Texas Jurisprudence

Down on the Brazos river, during the pioneer days of Texas, a country Negro rode his mule to town one Saturday afternoon. He came to the river, just opposite the town, and found it necessary to swim the stream which was swollen with the waters of recent rains.

Both the Negro and the mule made a successful landing on the other side and proceeded to the town. During the afternoon the Negro became intoxicated. Late in the afternoon when he attempted to cross the river again on his way home, the Negro fell from the horse, was drowned, and the body, with foot in the stirrup, dragged by the mule to the sand bank beyond.

When the coroner and justice of the peace appeared, he found a pistol upon the body of the deceased. After taking all facts into consideration, the officer of the commonwealth fined the dead Negro twenty-five dollars for unlawfully carrying a concealed weapon and took the mule to pay the fine.

Mandy: "Rastus, yo' makes me think yo' got the equator on yo'."

Rastus: "How cum, Mandy?"

Mandy: "Yo' got sech a hot line!"

PREMATURE DIAGNOSIS

To a plantation store, in the black belt of Mississippi, the Negroes had come on Saturday afternoon to purchase their supplies of tobacco and groceries. The store keeper was a white man who often sold second class merchandise at first class prices.

Among the customers was Rastus Johnson who brought back a ham which he had purchased the day before, and which he declared was not good. "Boss, it sho' am rancid," he said.

"That ham is all right, Rastus," insisted

the store keeper, "because it was cured only last week."

"Well, boss," said Rastus, "Ah doesn't b'lieve it wuz cured las' week, but if it wuz cured, it sho' has had a awful relapse!"

SILENCE IS GOLDEN

Sam and George, two Negro wood cutters, were constant companions and close friends, despite their occasional differences. Late in the afternoon one day their minds and emotions became more active as they neared the close of the day's labor.

Finally, Sam took serious exceptions to one of George's indolent and harmless remarks. As a consequence, Sam rebuked George for his stupidity. George said nothing in response.

Sam became more enraged and more profane than ever. George, still unconcerned, said nothing.

Then Sam, in his impetuosity, increased both the intensity and scope of censure upon his friend. George gave no answer to it all.

Again, Sam invoked a deluge of curses upon his companion. He called him all the names that an enraged mind could think of and that a fluent vocabulary could express. Still George said nothing.

This was more than Sam could endure. In final desperation, he exclaimed: "Look heah, Niggah, don't gemme no mo' ob yo' damned silence!"

WINSOME WILLIE

A Negro boy of jelly-bean appearance was employed to do certain forms of manual labor at a cafeteria. While on duty he had a long distance telephone call from one of the fair sex of his race. The proprietor willingly gave the young lover permission to talk from the business telephone.

After he had hung up the receiver, the Negro said with a triumphant air: "Ah speck Ah better go an' fin' out how much dat call wuz."

"Does your girl call you collect?" inquired the proprietor.

"No, suh, she always calls me Willie."

SCIENTIFIC DATA

A group of city residents were motoring through the country in southern Mississippi. Near the road they spied a Negro who had captured and dragged from the marshy water a furious alligator. Evidently, from his maneuvers, the Negro was familiar with the habits of his angry captive.

Naturally, the visitors stopped and asked many questions of the darkey about the alligator and his peculiarities. Finally, one of the party asked, "Is he amphibious?"

"Amphibious as hell," answered the Negro, "he eat yo' up in a minit!"

THE POWER OF PERSUASION

The pastor of the church, displaying eloquence, conviction, and profusion of knowledge, held his congregation spell-bound for two and one-half hours. His sermon was convincing, but Ephraim Johnson, a devout and critical member of the organization, was unable to follow part of the logician's argument.

"Bruddah Pastuh, dat sho' were a mighty pow'ful surman whut yo' preach, but Ah sho' don't dissimilate dat dare wuhd *phenomenon* whut yo' talk so much 'bout," said Ephraim.

"Well," said the pastor, "Ah'll jes' 'splain hit tuh yo'. 'Spose Ah's gwine down de road an' all at once Ah spies a cow layin' out by de side ob de road, jes' chewin' her cud an' switchin' her tail an' sayin' nuthin' jes' as low as she can. Bruddah, dat ain't no *phenomenon*."

"Den, ef Ah goes on down de road a little furder, an' lookin' way up on a thistle in de top ob a tree, Ah spies a little bird, jes' singin' lak its little heart would bust. Bruddah, dat ain't no *phenomenon*."

"Den, ef Ah goes on still furder, an' sees dat cow sittin' way up on a thistle in de top ob a tree, singin' lak a little bird, Bruddah Johnson, dat am a *phenomenon*."

Fighting for Peace

A middle-aged Negro of subnormal intelligence was brought before a police magistrate on a charge of fighting and otherwise disturbing the peace and dignity of the State. As the court interrogated him about the details of the affair, the darkey became very much excited as well as apologetic. The judge requested him to relate all the details of the fighting.

"Well, jedge, we wuz all down tuh Raz Johnson's at de chu'ch soci'ble. Some ob us wuz out in de back yahd jes' takin' a little choc beer whut de Sunday School Committee furnished. Den all ob a sudden dat no count Niggah, Sambo, ups an' calls me a damn, black fool, an' Ah draws back mah fis' an' hits 'im fo'teen times on de haid! Now, jedge, whut would yo' do ef he'd call yo' a damn, black fool?"

"But I am not black, and such a state-
ment would not be true," answered the
judge.

"Yeh, jedge, Ah knows yo' ain't no black
fool," said the offender, "but jedge, 'spose
he ups an' calls yo' de kin' ob a fool whut
yo' is!"

The Proof of the Pudding

Sampson Phillips had given considerable
trouble among the Negroes of the community where he resided. The police found it
necessary to arrest him one evening because
of a disturbance, and to place him in jail.
The next morning he was brought before the
police judge of the city court.

"Well, Sampson, here you are again; what
have you been doing this time?" asked the
judge.

"Ah ain't been doin' nuthin', jedge—Ah
swears 'fo' Gawd Ah ain't," pleaded the Negro.

"Then, what are you charged with?" demanded the judge.

"Jedge, Ah disremember zactly whut
dey calls hit, but wuz sumpin' dat sounded
tuh me lak 'fragrancy'."

Whereupon, the judge sniffed, frowned
deeply, and declared vehemently: "Guilty!
Ten days! Somebody raise all the windows
back there!"

POLITENESS AND TACT

Useless White, a perfectly black and kinky-headed Negro boy, applied to the manager of a Southern hotel for a position as bell hop. The latter informed him that he was badly in need of a boy but that he had to be careful in selecting those who conducted his guests to their rooms, ran errands for them, etc.

"For example," said the manager, "politeness and tact are especially necessary, and I would not employ any boy who does not possess these two qualities to a marked degree."

"Boss, dem's two things whut no Niggah ain't got no mo' ob dan Ah is. Mah p'liteness an' tac' am mos suttinly astoundin'," said Useless.

"You seem to know these terms; can you explain to me the difference between politeness and tact?" he inquired.

"Dat's de mos' simples' thing whut is," explained the Negro. "While Ah wuz wuhkin' down at de Elite Hotel, de boss say fuh me to go up tuh Room fo' seben an' fix de window in de baffroom. When Ah opens de do', dar wuz a real lady a settin' in de baff tub. Lawd! Ah jes' run out an' shet de do' an' say, "Scuse me, suh! 'Scuse me, suh!'. Dat *'scuse me'* wuz p'liteness, an' dat *'suh'* wuz tac'.""

THE LAST BENEDICTION

Lucius had been a bad Negro, and he had met a sudden and unexpected death. His body had been borne to the church where an elaborate funeral was being held. He had been the terror of the community, and no one could conscientiously speak a good word in his memory. It was with much difficulty that one of his acquaintances was persuaded to speak a few words about the departed brother. The oration was brief and the speaker's words were cautiously chosen, as follows:

"Ah would lak tuh say dis fuh Lucius— He wuz not always as bad as he sometimes wuz, an' Ah hopes he's gone whar Ah knows he ain't."

EMBARRASSING EXPOSURE

A colored bishop in Tennessee carried many responsibilities, with respect to both the temporal and spiritual affairs of his organization. Among the preachers of his diocese was the Reverend Ezekiel Jeremiah Jones, a pious but unpopular minister who could neither lead nor drive the membership of the flock assigned to him.

As a consequence, the Reverend Mr. Jones was having many ecclesiastical troubles, not the least of which was the collection of his own salary. He, therefore, wrote the bishop often about his plight, appealing eloquently for financial aid. When the bishop's patience became exhausted, he notified the pastor to make no further appeals to him for money.

After several months of silence, the church dignitary received the following communication from the distressed pastor:

"Dear Bishop: Dis heah ain't no appeal. Dis am a repo't—Ah ain't got no pants!"

HALF MOURNING

A Southern woman was visiting in New York City. Before leaving, she purchased presents for the several members of her family, including one for her colored maid. The present selected for the maid was a waist of bright red color. When she returned home, she found Lily clothed in black.

"Why, Lily," she said, "what misfortune has come upon you and your family?"

"Yo' see, Missus," said Lily, "mah thu'd husban' done died while yo' wuz gone."

"I'm sorry," said the woman. "I'll just give the waist to Malindy, and get something else for you."

"Nevah min,' Missus," answered Lily quickly. "Doan do dat. Hit sho' am a splendid cullah. Dat Niggah wan't much 'count nohow. Fum now on Ah'll jes' be in mo'nin fum de wais' on down!"

TAKING INVENTORY

A small Negro boy stepped into a downtown drug store and asked for permission to use the telephone. His intelligence, enthusiasm, and general demeanor attracted the attention and interest of the proprietor who listened to what he said:

"Hello, is dis Miz Pahker?—'Tis? Well, Mis Pahker, does yo' hab a little black niggah wuhkin' fuh yo' by de name ob Tobe Mosely?—Uh huh—Well, do he gib purfec' satisfaction?—He do? Den yo' don't want anudder boy in de place ob 'em?—Thank yo', Miz Pahker."

The boy hung up the receiver, moved his cap to the side of his head, and strutted proudly toward the door. "Are you lookin for a job, boy?" asked the proprietor of the store.

"Nossuh, Ah ain't lookin' fuh no job. Ah's de boy whut's wuhkin' fuh de lady—jes' checkin' up on mahse'f."

Courtship Without Acquaintance

Nancy Brown, a vivacious young colored woman, received much attention from young men admirers of her race. Her mother took great precaution to give Nancy the protection that her personal and physical charms demanded.

One evening when Mrs. Brown returned home, she observed her daughter resting complacently in the arms of a gallant young Romeo whose acquaintance the mother had never made.

"Nancy," said Mrs. Brown, "speak to dat good lookin' Niggah, an' tell him to remove dem ahms fum 'round yo' wais'."

"Tell 'em yo'sef," retorted Nancy. "He's a purfeck stranger tuh me!"

When Man Comes to Himself

It took considerable time for the colored minister to work his audience up to the point of proper ebulition and co-operation. When he did, the response was genuine, and a chorus of "amens" sustained him on every point.

The minister became eloquent as he portrayed the awful predicament of the Prodigal Son in a foreign land:

"Bredren, dat po' boy wuz way out to de

back ob de hawg pen, settin' on a rock, keepin' company wid his mis'ry, an' worryin' 'bout his sins. Den he couldn't stan' it no longah, an' he pulled off his hat an' frowed it 'way! Den he stuck his feet in de air, pulled off his shoes, an' frowed dem 'way! Den he riz up, pulled off his coat an' suit, an' frowed dem 'way! Den he pulled off his shirt, an' frowed it 'way!

"Den, Bredren, de po' boy come to hisse'f!"

IT COULD BE WORSE

A terrible wreck occurred on the logging railroad, and the Negro fireman was badly injured. After he was given medical attention and his pains alleviated as much as possible, the superintendent appeared to ascertain information about his relatives.

"Do you have a wife?" asked the superintendent.

"No suh, Boss, no suh, Ah makes mah own livin'," answered the injured man.

"And you have never been married in your life?" questioned the official.

Then the Negro replied sadly: "No suh, Boss, dis am de worstest fix Ah wuz evah in."

BONEHEAD SERVICE

A white man stepped into a short-order restaurant for his supper. Among the Negro waiters, he recognized at once an old acquaintance named Henry. The latter was a good waiter. He was extremely courteous, endeavored to please, understood human psychology, and was not averse to tips— both large and small.

Henry took the order, which included poached eggs, and promised quick delivery. As the Negro hurried out to fill the order, the man called to him and said:

"Henry, I've changed my mind about what I want to eat—just eliminate the eggs, please."

"Jus' do whut wid 'em?" asked Henry.

"Just eliminate them," answered the man.

"Now, Boss," said Henry, "we'd be jus' proud tuh 'liminate dem aigs fuh yo' an' fix 'em up 'zactly lak yo' wants 'em, but hit jus' cain't be did 'case we busted de 'liminator dis mawnin' befo' breakfus."

THE OTHER SOLDIER'S FEET

The Negro rookies, assembled in line, were told by the black sergeant that the inspection officer would soon arrive. He admonished them to be good soldiers, commanding them, with fire in his eyes, to assist him in making a good impression on the white officer. "Now, Ah wants all yo' Niggahs to fo'm a straight bee-line, an' when Ah sez 'eyes right', Ah wants to heah evah' Niggah's eyes click," he ostentatiously told them.

When the officer arrived he carefully surveyed the sphinx-like darkies standing at "attention." "Private Washington," he said, "move your feet back—they stick out too far in the front." With flashing eyes and with no small degree of excitement the scrawny little black promptly answered,

"Cap'n, skuse me, please suh, dem ain't mah feet, dem's Private Ivins's feet—he's behin' me."

THE LAW OF NATURE

Uncle Joe, an old-time antebellum Negro, was much beloved by the son of his former master. But Uncle Joe and his wife, Mandy, were not enjoying prosperity, and they had much difficulty in obtaining necessary food and clothing.

"Uncle Joe," said his white friend, "next Thursday is Thanksgiving. Take this dollar and go buy you and Aunt Mandy a turkey."

The Negro accepted the money with thanks and humility. Then he rushed home to convey the good news to his wife. Without equivocation, Mandy snatched the money from Uncle Joe and said:

"Jes' gemme dat dollah, Niggah, an' go an' git dat turkey in de natu'al way."

MODERN WIVES

George and Sam, close friends and companions in their youth, became separated for several years. During this time each had married. When they met, each indulged in gushing compliments to his wife as he endeavored to prove his own wife superior to the wife of the other. Finally, they touched the subject of feminine economy as a contributing force to conjugal happiness.

George: "Yo' know, mah wife is de mos' economicalest woman whut evah lived. Lemme tell yo' whut dat woman done—dat gal tuck one ob her ole dresses, tore hit up, an' made me a bran' new tie!"

Sam: "Shucks, Niggah, dat ain't nuthin'! Lemme tel yo' whut dat gal ob mine done—yo' know, she tuck one ob mah ole ties an' made herse'f a bran' new dress!"

Judas Iscariot

Marse Henry, down in the good old State of Georgia, had been riding over and inspecting his cotton farms. The day was sultry and the cotton had been "laid by." About eleven o'clock, thirsty from long riding, Marse Henry rode up to a cabin which was located in a cluster of tall trees shading the large family of lazy pickaninnies that lay stretched on the ground. He greeted Aunt Liza, the mother, told her that he was very tired and he would like to have a drink of cool water.

"Mos' suttinly, Marse Henry, yo' kin hab a cool drink ob watah. Judas Iscariot, git

de gemman a drink ob watah," said Aunt
Liza as she spoke in commanding tones to
her young Negro son who obeyed with unusual promptness.

"What did you call that youngster?" inquired Marse Henry.

"Judas Iscariot—dat's his name."

"Why did you call him Judas Iscariot?"

"Well, hit wuz jus' dis way," answered
Aunt Liza, "we tried tuh giv' 'em all Bible
names, an' dere wuz jus' natchly so many ob
'em dat de names all run out. So we didn't
name dat young un 'till he were a great big
boy, when one day Ah wuz readin' in de
Bible whar hit say 'Judas Iscariot, hit wuz
bettah you'd nevah been bawned,' an' I sez
dat's dat niggah's name."

JIM THE BAPTIST

Jim was an unusually black Negro. He
was industrious, dependable, and religious.
For several years he was superintendent of
the Sunday School. He disliked shams, was
opposed to new forms of worship, and possessed intense religious prejudices.

A white man engaged him in conversation
about a religious revival in the Methodist
Church. "What do you think about it?" he
asked him. "Well," said Jim, "de Bible hit

speaks ob John de Baptis', but hit don't say
nuthin' 'bout John de Methodist, do hit?"

"Then you must be a Baptist," said the
white man.

"Lemme tell yo' somethin'," said Jim.
"Whenevah yo' see a Niggah an' he ain't a
Baptis', somebody's been foolin' wid 'im.
Yas, suh, Ah sho' is a Baptis'. Ah's Baptis' tuh de core—Ah walks Baptis', an' Ah
talks Baptis', an' mah bon's jes' rattle Baptis'."

LOOKING THROUGH COLORED GLASSES

A devout church member happened to be
in Memphis, Tennessee, over Sunday. Following his usual custom, he arose early on
Sunday morning and made preparations to
attend church services as he always did at
home. He walked down Church Street in
the vicinity of a group of church buildings,
looking for the church of his choice.

Just as he was about to cross the street,
he observed an old Negro woman, hobbling
along the street and carrying a basket on her
arm. He decided to seek from her the information he desired.

"Auntie," he said, "can you tell me where
the Christian Church is?"

"Yas, suh," said the ancient Negro, "dey's
all Christian Chu'ches 'ceptin' dat li'l Camp-
bellite Chu'ch down dere on de co'ner."

CREATURES OF MATHEMATICS

The company of colored soldiers, clad in new khaki uniforms, stood at silent attention. The Captain, observing that one soldier several times raised his left hand to his head, rebuked him as follows:

"Private Johnson, keep your hand down by your side. Why do you keep scratching your head?"

Whereupon Private Johnson apologetically answered, "Cap'n, Ah's got 'rithmetic bugs on mah haid."

"Arithmetic bugs!" said the Captain. "Why do you call them arithmetic bugs?"

"Cap'n," he said, "Ah calls dem 'rithmetic bugs 'case dey adds tuh mah troubles, dey subtracts f'um mah pleasure, dey divides mah attention, an' dey multiplies lak de dickens!"

THE JOURNEY'S END

A Kentucky colonel came into possession of some very choice whiskey. He related all the circumstances to George, his long and faithful colored servant. Pouring a goodly quantity of the liquor into a glass, he passed it to George for his judgment as to the quality. The old Negro's face beamed with delight and appreciation as he gulped down the entire contents of the glass. The effect was soon evident, and George became very personal and confidential.

"Cunnel," said George, "when dey lays me out an' says Ah is daid, dey could be mistaken; an' Ah wants yo' to see dat dey don't bury no live Niggah. So Ah wants yo' to jes' git some good whiskey, tek a lit'l smidgin' ob hit on yo' fo'-finger, an' wave it back an' fo'th under my nose. An' ef Ah doesn't set right up in de coffin, jes' tell'm Ah is deceased an' tuh go ahaid wid de fun'ral."

DEEP RIVER

Rastus and Mandy were rowing in a boat late one evening, along a deep and tranquil river. As the moon beams pierced through the foliage of the trees and fell upon them, Rastus attempted to express his affections in a fond embrace. But Mandy resisted, time after time, this method of demonstrating their affection.

Finally, Rastus became desperate, resorting to threats of violence. "Mandy," he said, "ef yo' doan lemme kiss dem precious lips ob yo'rn, Ah's gwine'r upset dis heah boat in de middle ob de rivah!"

The next morning, Mandy told her mother

all about the experiences of the preceding evening.

"An' did yo' let de gemman kiss yo'?" inquired the mother.

"Well, now," answered Mandy, "did yo' see anything in de papah dis mawnin' 'bout two Niggahs drownin' in de rivah las' night?"

More Essential Than Ever

Jennie, the colored cook, requested an early leave one Sunday to attend a funeral. Clad in black, she left early in order that she might occupy an honored seat among the mourners of the occasion. From her point of view, the funeral was a complete success.

On the following Sunday, she requested another leave to attend a wedding. She had, of course, discarded the gloomy black of the previous Sabbath for the gayest attire she could obtain.

"Why, Jennie," said the white woman, "you know you were away only last Sunday. Is your presence absolutely needed at the wedding?"

"It am indeed mo' needed dan evah, Miz Lawson," answered Jennie emphatically. "Yo' see las' Sunday Ah was jes' a moanah fuh de cawpse; but dis Sunday Ah's gwine'r be de bride ob de cawpse's husban'."

FORENSIC ART

A great political campaign was in progress. The contest was between two political orators in the white primary election of a Southern State. People had come from several counties to pay homage to the candidates of their choice.

One of the candidates, an orator of great fame, paid a glowing tribute to the womanhood of the South. Then he gave eulogies to Jefferson Davis and to all the leaders and followers of the Southern Confederacy. The peroration came when, with eloquence and passion, he presented his own public record and commended all of his official acts as sane, wise, and statesmanlike.

While the orator was near this climax, two Negro boys happened to pass in the rear of the great throng of people. They stopped, listened intently to the speaker for a few minutes, then gazed at one another.

"Say, boy, who am dat man speakin'?" inquired one Negro of the other.

"Ah doesn't know who he am," replied the other, "but whoevah he am, he sho' do recommen' hisse'f mos' highly."

Old Timer: "Ef yo' don't know whar yo' is goin', why is yo' in sech a hurry?"

On With the Battle

Fifteen thousand Negro troops had been quietly moved to the front of a French sector assigned the Americans during the World War. Immediately behind them was a support of thirty thousand white American soldiers.

The sector had been quiet since the Negroes had been moved in. Only an occasional cannon shot was fired to impress all that the war was still going on. The Negroes had never participated in battle, and they were anxiously awaiting the first opportunity. Finally the word came that an advance was to be made at daybreak. On the night before, there were feelings of joy, mingled with no little anxiety among the Negro patriots.

"Amos," said a strutting corporal, "we is sho goin' ovah de top in de mawnin'. Jes' whut will be de headline of de papahs tomorrow when dey read 'bout dese black boys movin' in battle formation?"

"Ah'll tell yo' whut will be de headlines in de papah," answered Amos mournfully: *"Thirty Thousand White Soldiers Tromped tuh Death by Fifteen Thousand Retreatin' Niggahs!!"*

VISION VERSUS VILLAINY

Jerry and Jim, two successful Negro farmers, lived near each other in the cotton section of a Southern State. They were members of the same church and were fraternal brothers of the same lodge.

Their long friendship was considerably disturbed as a consequence of a financial transaction between them. After many conferences and after extolling the good qualities and high character of a certain mule that he owned, Jerry negotiated a sale of the coveted animal to Jim. The next morning Jim appeared with the mule at the cabin of Jerry and demanded a return of the money in exchange for the mule, claiming that the animal was completely blind. Jerry not only made a vigorous denial but claimed that the vision of the donkey had been tested and found perfect.

"Dat mule's blin'," said Jim. "Ah knows 'cause he run ovah de fences, knocked down de bahn do', couldn't see how to eat his vit'als, an' kicked de lit'l red ca'f wid bof feet! Dat mule's blin', Ah tells yo'—can't see hisse'f an' nuthin' else!"

"No, he ain't blin'," contended Jerry. "He jus' natu'ally don't give a damn!"

Book Names

Dinah, the new cook for a white family, appeared at her duties on the third morning accompanied with two neatly dressed pickaninnies.

"What are the names of your children?" inquired the white lady.

"De boy's name am Morphine an' de gal's named Opium," replied the cook cheerfully.

"Those are queer names," said the lady. "How did you happen to name them Morphine and Opium?"

"Law, Miz Po'ter, dem ain't queer names, dem's book names," answered the black mammy. "De book whut had de names say dat Opium an' Morphine am de product of de wild poppy; an' Miz Po'ter, ef de evah wuz two chillun dat had a wild poppy, dem two Niggahs has."

HALF LOAF BETTER THAN NONE

The Mount Zion Church of All Saints was poor in financial resources. But its membership possessed a growing spirit of progress.

As a consequence, the old pastor was discharged, and a committee was appointed to negotiate for procuring a preacher who held a D.D. degree. They were very promptly informed, by an American university, that such a person was available but that he would require a salary of fourteen hundred dollars.

After giving due consideration to the matter, the committee was instructed to write another communication to the effect that the salary of fourteen hundred dollars was twice as much as the church was able to pay. It hoped, however, to be able to pay more at an early date.

Therefore, the authorities were requested to send them a temporary pastor with only one D.

The Last Word

Jerry Washington, a country Negro, was standing trial on a charge of hog stealing. Although he stoutly asserted his innocence, a jury of twelve men adjudged him guilty and assessed his penalty at two years of hard labor in the State penitentiary.

"Jerry Washington," said the judge, "you are about to be sentenced to a term at hard labor in the penitentiary. Do you have anything to say before the sentence is passed upon you?"

"Ef de co't please, Ah has a few remahks," said Jerry. "Ah suttinly does thank de sheriff fo' de mos' kin' treatment whut he have gemme while Ah wuz in his custody. An', jedge, yo' has gemme a mighty nice trial. But, jedge, dem twelve men whut wuz on dat jury, dey sho' has done ruined dareselves wid me fo' evah mo'!"

The Morning After

After the Civil War Uncle Eben continued to live on the plantation of his former master. A great fondness and affection existed between them. They often talked of the happy days they had seen together, and as the infirmities of age approached, they con-

versed seriously about religion and the life
after death.

"Eben," said the former master, "if you
die first, I want you to come back and tell
me what it is like over there. And if I die
first, I'll come back and tell you what it is
like."

"Dat suits me, Massa," answered Uncle
Eben, "wid jes' a little providin', an' dat
providin' am dis: Ef yo' dies fus', Massa
John, Ah wants yo' tuh promise me right
now dat yo'll be sho' tuh cum back in de day
time an' not in de night time."

* * *

CUT OFF THE GAS

A Negro preacher, clad in a frock and high
collar that gave an odor of sanctity, was put-
ting on the "arousement" preparatory to a
big collection. Fortunately, the congregation was unaware of his designs.

"Breddern, dis chu'ch am gwine'r walk,"
cried the minister. "Let 'er walk, Bruddah,
let 'er walk!" responded the membership in
unctious tones.

"Breddern, dis chu'ch am gwine'r run,"
cried the preacher in still louder tones. "Let
'er run, Bruddah, let 'er run!" came the enthusiastic response.

"Breddern, dis chu'ch am gwine'r fly,"
echoed the vibrant voice of the leader. "Let

'er fly, Bruddah, let 'er fly!" came the hilarious reaction to this eloquence.

"But," said the preacher, "it am gwine'r take money tuh make dis chu'ch fly." There was general silence until there emanated from the amen corner the low and mournful words, "Jes' let 'er walk, Bruddah, jes' let 'er walk!"

Teaching the Ignorant

Sam and Mose, two Negro boys, had been drafted for military service during the World War. Both were strangers to the language of army routine.

On the second day after their arrival at the camp they were assigned duties at the Kitchen Police, popularly designated as K. P. duties. Their particular work was that of peeling potatoes. Later in the day, as the performance of this duty became irksome, Sam laid down his knife and began to talk to his companion, who continued his task with the usual speed.

"Mose," said Sam, "whut does dey mean when dey keeps on talkin' in dis army 'bout doin' K. P., doin' K. P.?"

"Look heah, big boy," answered Mose, "Good thing yo' ast 'bout dat! K. P., black boy, means Keep Peelin'! Keep Peelin'!"

SEA FOOD

On the banks of the Lower Mississippi stood the Negro cabin that had been occupied for years by Hez Hamilton and his family. The latter consisted of his wife, Eliza, and their numerous offspring of kinky-headed children whose ages varied from a few weeks to twenty years. Not even the parents knew the number.

A stranger who happened to be passing stopped to observe the playful antics of this large family of children. It seemed to him that they literally covered the river bank. Then to his surprise, he saw a vicious alligator creep up to the water's edge, swallow one of the pickaninnies, and disappear as suddenly as he had come.

The stranger approached the house, knocked on the door, and asked the Negro woman if she had missed any of her children.

"No suh, Ah ain't missed none uv 'em," she answered.

Then he told her what he had seen—the disappearance of the little dark morsel of alligator meat.

"'Liza," said Hez, "Ah has been tellin' yo' fer a long time dat sumpin' been gittin' dem chillun!"

SHUT THE DOOR

A Negro workman at Galveston, where the winters are exceedingly mild, had an unexpected opportunity to go to Chicago. He boarded the train hastily and within thirty-six hours was well near the point of his destination.

But he failed to anticipate the serious inconvenience of being in shirt sleeves and clad in the cotton garments of a Southern climate. Added to this inconvenience was the fact that it was the month of January and a terrible blizzard was raging around the Great Lakes. In Chicago the thermometer stood twenty degrees below zero.

Shivering as he got off the train, the Negro walked several blocks from the station. The bitter cold was too much for him, and he fell unconscious upon the icy sidewalk. He was soon picked up, pronounced dead, and borne away to the morgue where it was decided that cremation was the most convenient disposition of the body.

After the body had remained in the cremator the usual time, the attendants opened the door to remove the ashes of all that was mortal of this dusky son of the South. Whereupon, to their surprise, the Negro raised his head, blinked his eyes, and said: "Shet dat do'! Whose lettin' dat col' air come in heah!"

THE FIGHTING POINT

Sambo and his wife were standing trial on a charge of disturbing the peace on the preceding Saturday night. The judge placed Sambo under oath and requested him to relate all the facts connected with the unfortunate occasion.

"Well, Jedge, hit wuz jes' lak dis," said Sambo. "Me an' Liza gits into a argument ovah de washin' money whut she done takes in. Dat woman calls me a low down, triflin', wuthless Niggah, an' lams me ovah de haid wid de skillit. Ah riz up high an' bang a cha'r ovah de top ob her haid. Den mah wife th'owed a pot ob hot coffee in mah face, an' Ah ups again an' kicks her in de neck."

"Then what happened?" asked the judge.

"Well, suh, jedge, den bof ob us gits mad an' stahts tuh fightin'."

NORTH BOUND

A Negro youth, a shine boy, was a material court witness in a shooting affair that took place at a hotel.

"You say you heard the shooting?" asked one of the attorneys.

"Yas suh, Ah heah'd de shooting'—Ah sho did heah it," said the boy.

"How many shots were fired?" asked the attorney.

"Dere wuz two shots, Boss—one right aftah de udder—jus' like boom! boom!" answered the boy.

"Now, tell us where you were when the shooting occurred," requested the lawyer.

"Well, when de fus' shot wuz fired," said the boy, "Ah wuz down in de basement ob de hotel by de bahbar shop shinin' a gen'man's shoes, but Ah didn't do no mo' shinin'. Den when de secon' shot was fired, Ah wuz down 'bout fo' blocks by de depot goin' nawth!"

BURSTED BUBBLES

Rumors were in circulation that the bank was in a bad way. As a consequence, a long line of eager depositors were making a run on it. In this line one could not but observe the tall, gaunt form of Solomon Jackson who had stood in the crowded jam for two and one-half hours. The tellers continued to pay until Solomon arrived at the window to present his check when orders came suddenly to make no further payments. The indignant Negro demanded that his check, amounting to one dollar and seventy-five cents, be paid immediately. He was told that the bank was closed and that they could not pay him.

"Wha' fo' don't yo' gemme dat dollah an' six bits?" he demanded.

"Because the bank is busted. Didn't you ever hear of a bank going busted?"

"Yeh," said Solomon, "but Ah nevah did have one to jes' bus' right out in mah face befo!"

THANKS FOR THE BUGGY RIDE

After much persuasion the aviator prevailed upon Rastus to take a spin in the air. With quivering knees and chattering teeth the Negro reluctantly climbed into the plane. They ascended gradually until they were in the presence of the clouds. Then the machine went into a tail spin and performed all the other stunts that the aviator was capable of making. Finally they glided smoothly down to the earth and made a beautiful landing.

As he loosed himself and got out of the plane, the Negro was more excited than ever.

"Boss," he said, "Ah suttinly thanks yo' fuh dem two rides."

"But I haven't given you but one ride," said the aviator.

"Yeh, Boss, yo' has," replied the Negro. "Yo' has gemme mah fus' ride an' yo' has gemme mah las' ride."

THE ART OF DIPLOMACY

Among the Negroes that lived on the premises of a Southern planter was a preacher who possessed the subtle art of getting along with every one, white and black. One day the planter asked the preacher what subjects he usually preached on in his labors among his people.

"Oh, diffe'nt subjec's," answered the minister. "Sometimes Ah preaches on love, sometimes on babtism, sometimes on Hebben —jes' de pleasant subjec's dat makes 'em feel good."

"Why don't you preach occasionally on the subjects of chicken stealing and crap shooting?"

"Well, Ah tell yo', boss, when Ah preaches on dem subjec's hit allers throws a kin' ob coldness ovah de meetin'."

Mandy: "'Yo' reminds me ob one ob dem flyin' machines."

Rastus: "How come, woman, 'cause Ah is a high flyah?"

Mandy: "No suh, cullud boy, 'cause yo' ain't no use on earth!"

JUST BEGINNING

It was a hot summer day, after the crops were laid by. A baseball game between two teams of country Negroes was in full sway. The diamond had been laid off on level ground near a clump of elm trees adjacent to a cotton patch.

A group of white men, passing along a nearby road, were attracted by the enthusiastic demonstrations of the competing teams. They approached the scene of action just as a slim black was making a home run. Loud and boisterous yells indicated a victorious play. One of the visiting party asked the boy on first base what the score was.

"Sebenty-fo' tuh nothin'," came the reply.

"Seventy-four to nothing! They are beating you pretty bad, aren't they?" asked the visitor.

"Nossuh, dey ain't beatin' us," answered the black fan. "We ain't been in bats yit!"

EQUAL RIGHTS TO ALL

At the beginning of each service of the colored revival, individuals were given the opportunity to request special prayers of the congregation. Among these came the request of an old darkey that special prayers be offered for the floating kidneys of the world, this being a disease that had given the Negro much trouble and pain.

"But we can't do that," remonstrated the minister, "because we do not pray for interior troubles of that kind."

"Yas yo' does," retorted the darkey, "'cause las' night yo' wuz prayin' fuh all de loose livers in de chu'ch! De kidneys an' de livers am two organs whut's mouty close togedder!"

FINAL PERSEVERANCE OF THE SAINTS

The evening service of the colored revival was given to the hearing of personal testimonies. For the first time in many years Nathan had come to the church. As each testimony was followed by another, the burden of sin bore more heavily upon the heart of Nathan. Finally, when he could bear his conviction no longer, he arose and said:

"Breddern, Ah has been a awful mean Niggah! Breddern, Ah has got drunk, an' Ah has shot craps, an' Ah has stole chickens, an' Ah has tuck watah melons, an' Ah has used mah razo'! Breddern, Ah has done evah thing! But, thank God, Ah ain't nevah los' mah 'ligion!"

Harmony Restored

Beatrice, a colored cook for a white lady, was high tempered and a veritable autocrat in the kitchen. Despite these faults, she was efficient and reliable, and the lady considered her as indispensable to the management of the household.

One day she suddenly announced her resignation. She was to become a bride. Her mistress tried to dissuade her from the undertaking, telling her that an ugly temper like hers could result only in disaster. But Beatrice disregarded the advice, and the marriage took place as contemplated.

Reports of the couple's unhappiness followed immediately. Disagreements, quarrels, and blows ensued daily. After a few months, the lady happened to meet Beatrice one day down in town.

"I hope you and your husband don't quarrel any more," she said.

"We sho'ly doesn't do dat no mo'."

"That's fine. What caused you to stop it?"

"He's daid!"

A Unanimous Call

The time had come for the annual election of a pastor of the Ebenezer Baptist Church. Because of the opposition to the retention of the pastor, the entire membership was present to participate in its business affairs and to guarantee the continued supremacy of democratic rule. Anticipating the organized effort to depose him, the preacher decided not to relinquish the chair during the business session.

"Bredren an' Sistern," he said, "we is met to 'lect de pastuh ob dis chu'ch fuh anudder yeah. Dem dat's in favah ob keepin' me fuh de pastuh say 'Ah'!"

There was complete silence to the proposi-

tion. Whereupon, the minister said:
"Silence gives consent, an' Ah is yo' pastah. De Babtists am adjourned."

Not Enough Negro

Toward the close of a hot day in the month
of August, a good-natured Negro boy consulted a physician for a peculiar sensation in
his ears. An examination disclosed that
both ears were filled with water.

"How did it happen?" asked the physician.
"Have you been in swimming every day?"

"Nossuh, been eatin' watah milyan evah
day an' evah night," answered the boy with
a grin.

"Then your trouble is that there was too
much melon!" observed the doctor.

"Nossuh, not 'nough Niggah!" retorted
the youth with a still broader grin.

Catering to the Public

Among the more generous friends of
Dave Solomon, an indolent darkey, was a
prominent doctor. In exchange for the service of doing small jobs about his yard, the
doctor gave his old and discarded clothes to
Dave. The chief difficulty lay in the fact that

the doctor was low and fat, whereas the Negro was tall and slim.

One day Dave appeared in a pair of the doctor's old trousers which, despite the most liberal alterations, were much too short for him. Notwithstanding this, the Negro persisted in rolling up the legs of the dilapidated garment.

"Why," asked the doctor, "do you turn up the trousers when they are already too short?"

"Well, suh, boss, de psyrology ob de matter am dis: when Ah turns up dem britches laigs dey ain't nobody whut's gwine'r know dat dey am already too short fuh me."

WATCHFUL WAITING

Dinah, the colored cook, had been a faithful servant. But one day she suddenly announced her resignation to become the bride of Wash Potter, a new-comer who had made his appearance in the community just the week before.

"Dinah," said the mistress, "I owe you seven dollars, and here's another seven dollars as a wedding present."

"Miz Connah, would yo' min' keepin' dis heah fo'teen dollahs a while fuh me?" asked the confiding servant.

"Certainly not, Dinah," agreed the woman, "but since you are getting married, won't you need all your money?"

"Miz Connah," answered Dinah emphatically, "does yo' think Ah's gwine'r trus' mahse'f an' all dat money wid a puffeckly strange Niggah!"

NOT SLEEPING SICKNESS

A Negro boy settled himself comfortably in his seat on a local train and soon went soundly to sleep. A white man, passing through the coach and observing that the boy's mouth was quite wide open, mischievously placed a quantity of quinine on the Negro's tongue. As the quinine slowly dissolved, the boy began to move about and blink his eyes. Then he swallowed once, jumped suddenly from his seat, and ran frantically through the train yelling for a doctor.

"I am a doctor," said a man. "What's the matter with you?"

"Oh, Doctah! Oh, Doctah!" ejaculated the Negro, "Ah doesn't know all whut am de mattah! But, oh, Doctah, Ah's mouty sick, Ah's 'bout tuh die—cain't yo' do sumpin fuh me? Oh, Doctah, Ah doesn't know, but Ah is mos' sho' dat mah gall's busted!"

A Light Sentence

A prominent citizen and land owner had been brutally murdered by a Negro fiend in a certain section of Kentucky. The mob spirit prevailed, and the Negro was overpowered and hung on a high limb in a cluster of trees where he was captured.

As the participants of the mob were about to disperse, they observed another black crouched beneath a pile of brush within a few feet of the scene of the lynching. Though innocent of any connection with the murder, the latter had secluded himself in the hope of protection against the indiscretions of an enraged public. The leaders wanted no witnesses to their own act of lawlessness, so they asked if he had seen anything at all, to which came the reply, "Nossuh, frien's, Ah nevah seed nuthin'."

Then they asked what he thought about it all. Gazing intently upon the black bullet-ridden form which dangled in the air from the top of the tree, he said:

"Looks tuh me lak he got off mouty light!"

Boss: "Say, Rastus, why do you have that mule hitched up backwards?"

Rastus: "Boss, when Ah has dis mule hitched up right, he won't go any way 'cept backwards. So Ah jes' hitched him up backwards, an' now he backs frontwards!"

HOME, SWEET HOME

There were no soldiers, during the World War, who appreciated their American citizenship more than the colored boys who went over seas.

Early one morning a transport vessel, loaded with a contingency of returning Negro troops, appeared in New York harbor. As the boat glided smoothly toward the dock, all the troops were on the deck, eager to get a glimpse of their native land. They greeted everybody and everything with enthusiastic cheers.

Among the soldiers on the deck was a tall, sober Negro who gazed earnestly at the Statue of Liberty and spoke as follows:

"Ole gal, Ah's done looked into yo' face fuh de las' time, an' yo' is done looked at me fuh de las' time onless yo' turns yo' se'f 'roun' an' looks de udder way."

VERBAL INSPIRATION

The pastor of the Mount Zion Baptist Church was observed with his arms around a comely, chocolate-colored widow, a member of his flock. For this indiscretion, the preacher was brought to a church trial, charged with unbecoming conduct.

Admitting the charge, the minister stepped

to the pulpit and exclaimed: "Bruddahs an'
Sistahs, Ah is surprised at yo' ign'ance ob
de Scriptures! Ain't yo' nevah read in de
Good Book whar de Lawd Jesus took de lam's
ob his flock in his ahms an' blest 'em! Is
yo' gwine'r refuse yo' pastuh de pleasuah
ob imitatin' his Lawd by takin' a occasional
lam' tuh his bosom!"

The committee appointed to consider the
matter, after long deliberation, returned
with these resolutions: "Wheahfo', ouah
pastuh finds dat in ordah tuh imitate his
Lawd Jesus he mus' take a occasional lam'
tuh his bosom; Be hit resolved by de Mount
Zion Babtis' Chu'ch dat we accords ouah
servant dis privilege; But be hit also resolved dat heah aftah he shall always selec'
fuh dis pu'pose one ob de Ram Lam's."

FINANCIAL WIZARDS

Down in Mobile, Alabama, a group of Negroes organized a private bank. Among the
larger depositors was an industrious Negro
who bought and sold mules. His business
carried him to a smaller town in the State.
While in that town, he established business
connections at a bank operated by white people. The latter were convinced of the Ne-

gro's honesty, as a result of which they cash-
ed a check for $300.

In due time, the check was returned with
the usual notation, "No funds." The Negro
insisted that there was something seriously
wrong. Believing the Negro to be honest,
the officials of the bank wrote a scathing rebuke to the officials of the Negro bank for
returning the check of a depositor who had
money to his credit.

Then, they received the following answer
from the officers of the Negro bank:

"Whut we meant wuz dat de *bank* didn't
hev no funds. Now we has funds an' we is
paying de check."

BLUE SKY AVERAGE

A man who was traveling on a Pullman
was nearing the end of his journey. The
courtesies of the black porter increased ma-
terially at this particular time.

As the porter brushed the clothes and
shoes of the man, the latter was endeavoring
to determine upon the appropriate tip for
the service rendered. He, therefore, asked
the porter the amount of his average tip.
The porter replied that the average was one
dollar.

When the man handed him this amount,

the Negro caressed the silver coin affectionately as he said:

"Yas, suh, boss, but yo' is de fust pusson whut has come up tuh de av'rage!"

STRICT OBEDIENCE

During the oil boom in Wichita County, Texas, in 1919, a somewhat inebriated driller boarded the Pullman out of Fort Worth, at eleven p. m., and gave strict instructions to the porter to awaken him and put him off at Wichita Falls. "Hic! Porter," he said, "here's a dollar. Put me off at Wichita Falls. Now I'll be sleepy and I'll cuss you, and maybe I'll fight you; but don't pay no 'tention to them things—just put me off."

Next morning the driller awoke about nine o'clock, and found he had passed Wichita Falls by over two hundred miles. In a rage he rang for the porter and exclaimed: "Say, you d—d black rascal, why didn't you put me off at Wichita Falls like I told you?"

Both the porter's eyes and his entire face were covered with bruises. In a surprised way he looked the driller over, scratched his head, and said:

"Ah wondah who dat gen'man wuz dat Ah did put off!"

TAKE THE WITNESS

Malindy Brown, an old black mammy, was the star witness for the State in a murder case. After giving direct testimony, she was put under cross examination by the lawyer for the defense.

"Your name is Malindy Brown?"

"Whut yo' ast me dat fuh? Yo' knows mah name well as Ah does," she retorted.

"I believe you said your husband was hit in the fracas."

"No, suh, Ah didn't say dat—Ah said dat Niggah wuz hit on de haid!" she answered.

"Did you swear, a few minutes ago, that————"

"White folks!" interrupted Malindy, "Ah is a sistah in de chu'ch, Ah is, an' 'fo' Gawd Ah nevah swears tuh nobody!"

"Then did you say, a few minutes ago, that Lim Johnson, the deceased, was————"

"Nossuh," again interrupted the woman, "Ah didn't say nuthin' 'bout Lim Johnson bein' diseased!"

"Well, did you say that Lim Johnson was shot somewhere between the diaphragm and the medulla oblongata?"

"Stop yo' fool questions!" answered Malindy indignantly. "Ah said dat Niggah wuz shot 'tween de hawg-pen an' de chicken-house!!"

A Disciple of Blackstone

A darkey had been arrested and placed in jail for stealing chickens. While in jail he was permitted to have a private conference, preliminary to a trial, with his attorney. The lawyer was endeavoring to find what grounds of defense he could make for his client.

"Can you prove an alibi?" asked the attorney.

"How's dat, boss, can yo' prove de whut?"

"An alibi. That means can you prove

where you were at the time the offense was committed?" explained the lawyer.

"Jedge, dat's jes' whut Ah's skeered dey's gwine'r do."

ONLY PARTIAL PUNISHMENT

Mose and Rastus were neighbors who lived on adjoining town lots in the suburbs of Solomon Hill. Bitter feeling developed between the two households because of the depredations of a rooster that belonged to Mose. As a consequence, the poor rooster lost his life in the manner shown by the following conversation:

Rastus: "Looka heah, Niggah, Ah done tole yo not to shoot mah roostah, ain't Ah?"

Mose: "Yeh, an' Ah done tole yo' to keep yo' roostah outen mah gahden, too, ain't Ah?"

Rastus: "Dat roostah wuzn't in yo' gahden, Niggah. He jes' had his haid an' neck through dat crack in de fence."

Mose: "Well, dat's all I shot wuz his haid an' neck!"

First Negro: "How is yo' gittin' 'long wid de 'rithmetic?"

Second Negro: "Well, de figgers is givin' some trouble, but Ah is already learned to add up de oughts."

Lead Kindly Light

The Negro school at Soup Holler was dismissed frequently because no Socrates could direct the obstreperous youths who did not attend it for the purpose of acquiring useful knowledge. Knock-downs were common, razors were used naturally, Bedlam reigned, and no Ichabod was ever known to preside more than a week in the would-be Temple of Knowledge.

Then came along Professor Ezra Snow, a diminutive black of determined eye. One week, two weeks, three weeks—all passed and not a word of complaint about the intellectual leader of the community. A member of the school board decided to find out for himself. When he arrived he was astounded to find perfect order and studious pupils.

"How did you do it?" he inquired anxiously.

"I always knew," said the erudite Professor Snow, "that a Negro's greatest weakness is eating. Therefore, when a pupil is mean, I just eat his lunch. As long as my stomach holds out, I'll be a successful schoolmaster!"

Sergeant: "Whut is a fortification?"
Private: "Ah says dat a fortification am two twentifications!"

THE COURT KNOWS

A colored youth was brought into a juvenile court where he was adjudged an incorrigible. The evidence convinced the judge that the waywardness of the erring urchin was due largely to a lack of proper training.

Resenting what she considered an undeserved censure, the indignant mother reproachfully asked:

"Jedge, mout Ah ast dis question?"

"What is it?" inquired the court.

"Jedge," she said, "Ah knows yo' knows whut yo' knows yo' knows. But jedge, wuz yo' evah de parent ob a puffeckly wuthless cullud chile?"

EXCESSIVE ELUCIDATION

The Reverend Mr. Wheatley, pastor of a Negro church, was given to the use of big words and complicated discourse. But interest in the church lagged, the crowds became smaller, and collections decreased. Finally, a committee called on the minister and requested his immediate resignation. The preacher did not receive the committee kindly.

"Doesn't Ah argify? An' doesn't Ah sputify? An' doesn't Ah catechise?" contended the divine.

"Yo' sho' does do all dem things an' den some," the committee assured him.

"Den, wherefo' yo' doesn't demand no mo' ob mah preachin'?" he insisted. To which, the spokesman of the committee answered with emphasis.

"Bruddah Wheatley, yo' sho' does argify, yo' sho' does sputify, an' yo' sho' does catechise; but de trouble am dat yo' jes' simply doesn't show wherein!"

SILENT SILAS

Silas, a very talkative Negro, was brought before a magistrate's court down in South Louisiana. At the minute of his appearance in the court room, Silas insisted upon talking to the court about the case. Several times he began to talk, and each time the judge requested him to refrain.

"Just cut out your oratory, Silas, until you are sworn," admonished the judge. "Silas, do you promise to tell the truth, the whole truth, and nothing but the truth, so help you God?"

"Ah does, boss," said the Negro.

"Now go ahead with your testimony," requested the court.

"Well, jedge, wid all dem limertations yo' has jes' gemme, Ah doesn't b'lieve Ah hasn't nuthin' mo' tuh say atall."

Business Reverses

Uncle Tom was making an appeal to a white man for a gratuity. The latter had known the Negro, in a casual way, for several years, and he was much surprised at his new means of livelihood.

"Why, Uncle Tom, you don't mean to tell me that you have at last taken up begging?" inquired the white man.

"Yas, suh, boss, Ah ain't got no udder way gittin' 'long," answered the darkey.

"Why you once told me that you had a good business."

"Boss, Ah did have a good bizness— a one-han' laundry—but Ah's done los' mah bizness."

"How did you come to lose it, Uncle Tom?"

"Well, suh," replied Uncle Tom, "de way hit wuz, she jes' up an' divo'ced me!"

All About Nothing

Abe, a thoroughly hen-pecked husband of middle age, had given much thought to a reorganization of his household. But the ill temper and the biting tongue of Nancy always made him hesitate. Encouraged by the advice of a bachelor friend, Abe finally decided upon the undertaking. Returning home one evening, he blustered in, slammed the door, and said:

"Nancy, Ah ain't keepin' silent an' sayin' nuthin' no longah! Fuh once, Ah gwine'r up an' speak mah whole min'!"

"Yeh," retorted Nancy, "an' when yo' does speak yo' whole min', de big silence will suttinly be awful embarrassin'!"

Poor White Trash

Down in Georgia, where the rivers are narrow and swift-flowing, a Negro operated a toll ferry boat.

A shiftless and roving white man appeared with his family in a covered wagon and asked for free transportation across the river. But the Negro insisted that the cost was only a dime. The white replied that he would be glad to pay, but that he did not even have the dime. Whereupon, the darkey answered philosophically:

"Boss, ef yo' ain't got no mo' money dan dat, yo'll be 'bout as well off on dis side ob de creek as on de udder side."

White Friend: "How does this man look?"

Negro: "He look jus' lak de undah side ob a nickel watah milyun!"

CONFIDENTIAL ADVICE

A down-and-out stepped sluggishly into a restaurant early one morning for breakfast. One of the polite colored waiters came to take his order.

"All I want this morning are some kind words and some eggs," said the guest.

The waiter left promptly, reappearing in a few minutes, with the following sympathetic and confidential advice:

"Boss, heah's de aigs, an' de kin' wuhds is, *'Don't eat 'em'.*"

A VITAL MISTAKE

A Negro minister delivered a sample sermon to a new congregation. For the reason that his name was under consideration for the pastorate, members of the congregation were very observant, and even critical, of every talent and trait of the anxious preacher. They did not even exempt the social graces. When the services were over and his temporary stay in the community ended, the church postponed action in the case. He returned home in a dejected mood, relating the situation to his wife as follows:

"De preachin' on Sunday mawnin' wuz mouty pow'ful an' we had de Debil stahtin' on a long run. Den we went down tuh Bruddah Johnsing's fuh dinnah. We wuz settin' 'roun' de table an' evahthin' wuz jes' lairpin. Den Bruddah Johnsing say, 'Pahson, won't yo' hab some ob de cawn?' Hit wuz right heah, 'Liza, dat de Lawd fo'sook me, 'case Ah made a awful mistake an' passed mah glass."

TIME DID NOT HEAL

"Whiskey Joe" was so named because he was suspected of being the handy man of the bootleggers in the town. Despite these suspicions, Whiskey Joe always appeared immaculately dressed and was a social lion among the chocolate colored belles of the Negro community.

One day he appeared on the streets with swollen eyes, with a bandage across his forehead, and with other evidences of bad physical contact. A young white man questioned him as to the cause of this condition.

"Ah wuz bes' man at a frien's weddin', an' he smashed me up 'cause Ah kissed de bride," said the young Negro.

"But I thought," answered the white man, "that it was the custom for the best man to kiss the bride after the ceremony."

"Yeh," replied Whiskey Joe, "but dis wuz two yeahs aftah de ceremony!"

RECITING HIS LESSON

An atrocious murder had been committed. The trial had been conducted orderly, the death penalty had been assessed, and the gaunt youth of color was now about to pay the extreme penalty at a public hanging.

As the sheriff adjusted the noose about his neck, the prisoner was asked if he had anything to say.

"Yas, suh, Boss, Ah does. Dis heah sho' has taught me a good lessen, an' Ah trusts evahthin' tuh a all-wise an' unscrupulous Providence."

FIFTY-FIFTY

A traveling man, on the way between two cities in a Southern state, gave the Negro porter what was left of a pint of modern Volstead Whiskey in return for extra services. The next morning, when the porter came to brush his clothes, he said: "Well, George, how was that whiskey I gave you?"

With a broad grin on his face, George said: "Jes' right, boss, jes' right!"

"What do you mean by 'just right'?" asked the traveling man.

"Well, boss, hit's jes' lak dis," answered the porter. "Ef hit had a been any bettah, yo' wouldn't a gib hit tuh me; an' ef hit had a been any wuss, Ah couldn't a drunk hit."

The Last Call

The patient, Lem Johnsing, hovered between life and death with a burning fever. The colored physician gave another treatment and made another examination, while the patient's wife anxiously awaited the report.

"Well, Miz Johnsing," said the physician as he came from the sick room, "Ah sho' has done knocked de fever outen 'em fo'evah mo' dis time."

"Sho' nuff! Den do dat mean he am gwine'r git well, Doctah?" came the reply.

"No'm, Miz Johnsing," answered the doctor, "he ain't nevah gwine'r git well no mo', but yo' will hab de satisfaction ob knowin' dat he *died cured.*"

Something Wrong

Several of the Negroes of the neighborhood had been observing the peculiar antics of Alec Jackson. Through the moonlight they could see him as he ran back and forth, carrying in his hands a spoon and a bottle. During all of the following night, they observed he continued to run as he did the night before. On the third night, he

would skip back and forth, still clinging to
the spoon and bottle.

Such performances in the dead of the
night gave the Negroes much concern, caus-
ing the circulation of reports that Alec had
gone crazy. So they sent a committee to in-
vestigate. The committee first sought information from Alec's wife who said that
he had been ill but that he was much better.
Then they told her of his peculiar acts during each of three successive nights.

"Hit's de doctah dat make 'im ac' lak dat,"
said Mirandy. "De doctah gib 'im de medi-
cine an' tol' 'im tuh take hit two nights running', den skip one."

SHADES OF DEMOSTHENES

A Negro met an old time friend on the
streets of an Alabama town. It was eight
o'clock in the evening, and his friend was
wearing a dress suit, new shoes, and a derby
hat perched on the side of his head. All gave
evidences of unusual prosperity.

"Sambo, yo' sho' mus' hab some swell job
tuh dress up lak dat."

"Job!" said Sambo, "Mor'n dat, Ah's got
a perfession! Ah's a orator!"

"A orator! Whut am a orator, Sambo?"

"Yo' doan know whut hit am?" said Sam-

bo. "'Spose yo' wuz tuh ast a ordinary Niggah how much wuz two an' two—he'd jes'
say 'fo'.' But when yo' ast one ob us orators
how much wuz two an' two, he'd say dis wid
purfeck denunciation: 'When in de co'se ob
human events hit become necessary to take
de numeral ob de secon' awder an' add hit
to de figur' two, Ah says unto yo' widout
equivocation, an' wid malice toward none,
an' widout fear ob unsuccessful contradic-
tion dat de inevitable resul' am fo'.' Dat's
whut Ah is—a orator."

Flow Gently Sweet Afton

Reverend Josephus Jeremiah Watkins
spoke eloquently for more than two hours on
the evils of alcoholic beverages. Despite the
fact that only a few of his flock emitted unctious grunts of approval, the eloquence of
the minister reached its pinnacle at the close
of the sermon.

"Ah wish," he said exhaustively, "Ah had
all de choc beer an' all de unscriptural wine
an' all de undamnable whiskey in the whole
world, Bruddahs. Ah would pour all de
filthy foam into one great big rivah ob Sin!!
Let's hab de closin' song, Bruddahs an' Sistahs. An' let evahbody sing loud!"

Whereupon, the choir leader took charge
of the services and everyone joined lustily in-
singing "Shall We Gather At the River?"

QUIT WORRYING

Two Negroes were discussing the bad effects of worry upon the mind and the body. Both agreed that worry should be avoided, but they differed as to the manner of obviating it.

"Sambo, yo' know Ah ain't nevah gwine'r worry no mo'. Ah done got anudder Niggah to do all mah worryin' fuh ten dollahs a day," said Mose.

"But yo' don't make no ten dollahs a day. How is yo' gwine'r pay hit?" inquired Sambo.

"Dat's de fus' thing he's gotta worry 'bout," answered Mose.

More Chicken

The colored bishop was presiding with
great dignity at the chicken banquet given
in honor of the presiding elders who had
come from districts far and near. As a
group, the visitors gave ample outward evidence that they were capable of directing
the spiritual affairs of their respective com-
munities. They were large, fat and sleek,
showing that they had not wanted the temporal things in life. The only exception was
the Reverend Jeremiah Johnson, who was
small in stature, exceedingly black, and in-
significant in personal appearance.

As the banquet progressed, the spirit of
harmony, hilarious feeling, and brotherly
love increased with the quantity of whole-
some food served. Suddenly, the bishop observed that the Reverend Jeremiah Johnson,
seated far down the table and almost hidden
by the corpulence of others near him, was
not eating. "Brudder Johnson," he said,
"won't yo' have some mo' chicken?"

"Mo'!" said Reverend Johnson, "Mo'! Ah
ain't nevah had some, yit."

Razzer: "So you are raising wood-peck-
ers. What do you expect to do with them?"

Rastus: "Ah is usin' dem to 'liminate de
wood fum de wood alcohol!"

A Clandestine Enemy

Sam was very much agitated as he came to see an attorney. The latter had occasionally employed him to keep his yard.

"Sam," said the attorney, "you seem very much disturbed. Are you in trouble?"

"Yeh, Boss, Ah sho' is in a mighty lot ob trouble," replied Sam. "Dis mawnin', Ah gits a lettah fum a man whut say he gwine'r shoot me ef Ah doesn't stop stealin' his chickens. Boss, dis am awful, an' Ah is terrible skeered."

"But all you have to do, Sam, is to quit stealing his chickens—then you'll be in no danger," answered the lawyer.

"Yeh," retorted Sam, "but it don't say whose chickens dey is—it am one ob dem unanimous lettahs widout no name on it."

Service Above Self

Pete Patterson, a good humored colored boy, was temporarily attached to a group of American soldiers on the Argonne front. He was told that he would be expected in two hours to assume guard duty on the outpost. Pete protested that he was ill and that he just couldn't go.

The white sergeant brought in some

French gin and gave a liberal quantity to the sick soldier. This was followed shortly by another swig. The healing was immediate, and the Negro insisted that he go on duty at once, that an hour or two made no difference to him.

They crawled to the outpost, and whispered orders were given to the soldier. By this time, the gin had taken full effect, and Pete became hilarious. Standing up boldly he cried out: "Come on, yo' Guhmans! Ah's come clean 'cross de 'Lantic Ocean to see yo'! Come on, yo' Squa'-haids, come on!"

About that time a shell burst in the vicinity of the outpost. His comrades rushed under cover to determine what had happened. They found Pete sprawled out and unconscious, though not dead. First aid was administered, and as Pete came to, he rolled the whites of his eyes round and round, then said feebly:

"Dar's one thing 'bout dem Guhmans— dey sho' does gib yo' promp' servis."

———

Bruddah Brown: "Bruddah Most High Exalted Ruler, Ah thinks we needs a cuspidor in dis lodge."

Exalted Ruler: "Ah thinks so too. Bruddah Brown, Ah appoints yo' as *Cuspidor* of dis lodge!"

OBSERVING THE PROPRIETIES

Mose Johnson blew into town Sunday afternoon, a complete stranger in the community. At the station he accidentally met Malindy Brown who sympathized with the lonely stranger and invited him to enjoy the hospitality of her home during the evening. Mose was gallant, Malindy courteous. The first hour passed quickly, and there was prospect of a closer acquaintance.

"Malindy, ef yo' doesn't min', would yo' please——?"

"Stop, Mose Johnson!" interrupted the young woman. "Doan yo' git so fresh an' familiar. Mah name's Miss Brown. Ah doesn't 'low nobody 'ceptin' mah mos' pa'ticlah frien's tuh call me Malindy."

"Ah begs yo' pahdon, Miss Brown," replied Mose politely. "Ef yo' doesn't min', would yo' please shif' yo'se'f tuh de uddah knee? Dis one's gittin' tired."

BLACK SAYINGS

Liza: "Whut is yo' gwine do wid dat razor?"

Rastus: "See dem two shoes undah de baid. If de ain't no man in 'em, Ah is gwine tuh shave!"

Bad, Worse, and Worst

"Well, whut's de mattah wid yo' now?" a friend asked Rufus Jackson.

"Ah's a sick man," answered Rufus. "Fo' weeks ago de doctah tole me Ah hed 'berculosis an' dat hit couldn't be no worse. An' week 'fo' las' hit wuz mo' worser dan evah 'case he say Ah got two 'berculosis."

"Dey ain't no justis' no mo'," wailed Rufus. "Ah's sho' sick, an' Ah guess Ah's gwine'r die, 'case dat ain't all Ah got. Yistiddy de doctah say mah veins is too close— dat Ah got very close veins, an' de only he'p fuh me am tuh eat nuthin' else but chicken broth an' stay in nights. Ah tells yo', Sambo, bof' ob dem two things jes' cain't be did by one Niggah!"

On A Cold Trail

Ebon Thompson had not lived the most upright life, and the members of his own race did not speak kindly of him. Especially had his reputation for truth and veracity suffered severely in recent years. But a great revival of religion was in progress among the darkies, and many of the bad ones were being brought into the Baptist Church.

Among the converts was Ebon Thompson who was reluctantly accepted as a candidate for baptism. Despite the cold weather, it was decided that the ordinances should be administered immediately. The Negroes had assembled upon the banks of the creek, the ice had been broken, and the shivering converts led into the water. As Ebon emerged from the water, one of the deacons inquired, "Brudder Ebon, is yo' col'?"

"No suh, Ah ain't col'," said Ebon.

"Duck him agin, Pahson, he's still lyin'," retorted the devout deacon.

FOR VALUE RECEIVED

A gentleman of color called at the office of an attorney to ascertain the details of procuring a divorce. The lawyer expressed surprise and told the Negro he thought his home was a happy one. Pressed for an explanation, the Ethiopian admitted that he desired the divorce in order that he might marry another woman.

Then the lawyer told the darkey that it was unfortunate that he should be put to so much expense, which would be at least thirty dollars, and probably more. The Negro expressed great surprise at the cost. Finally, after much deliberation, he said:

"Boss, jes' nevah min' 'bout dat divo'ce. Dey ain't thirty dollahs wuth ob diff'rence 'tween dem two black gals."

NOT GUILTY

The Negroes of the South have an inherent feeling that the world owes them a living, and that food, like the water and the air, are necessities which no one has a right to deny them. Especially do chickens belong to this classification, as the following dialogue will illustrate:

Judge: "Rastus, are you the defendant in this case?"

Rastus: "Nossuh, Ah's de boy whut stole de chicken."

Judge: "Are you guilty or not guilty?"

Rastus: "Not guilty, jedge."

Judge: "Have you ever been in jail?"

Rastus: "Nossuh, jedge, Ah ain't nevah stole nuthin befo'."

AMERICA, THE BEAUTIFUL

After the Armistice was signed in November, 1918, every hamlet of the country had its quota of soldiers returning from over seas. Among these was Nicodemus Jefferson who lived in a small Mississippi town. Nicodemus, though glad to get back to his Southern home, was proud of his military

record and was given to no small amount
of boasting.

"What rank did you have in the army?"
asked his white employer.

"Ah wuz mos' gen'rally in de rear rank,"
he answered.

"What did you do in France and Ger-
many?" inquired the white man.

"Well, suh, one night de fus' sahgent tuck
me way out in 'No Man's Lan' an' puts me
on guard," said Nicodemus. "Den de sahgent sez, ef anythin' moves out dar, yo'
shoot! Yeh, Ah sez, an' ef anythin' shoots
out dar, Ah's gwine'r move!"

One Flag and One Interpretation

The Negro pastor preached an eloquent
sermon, during which time he used the word
"monotony" several times. After the sermon the members, especially the sisters,
congratulated him on the power of his mes-
sage.

"But," they said, "dey's one wu'hd—dat
wu'hd 'monotony' whut yo' use so much—
dat we doesn't git de full solemnity ob."

"Well, mah deah sistahs," said the pastor,
"Ah'll jes' illustrate de meanin' ob hit.

F'rinstance, ef er man hab sev'al wives, dat am polygamy; ef he hab two wives, dat am bigamy; but ef he hab jes' one wife, w'y dat, mah deah sistahs, am monotony."

PIETY BOILED DOWN

Irving Cobb tells the story of a prominent churchman who went from the North to spend a vacation on the Virginia plantation of a friend. Next morning he was awakened by the beautiful strains of "Nearer, My God, to Thee," which he traced to the kitchen where a fat, elderly Negro woman chanted the familiar words of the old gospel song.

"I am indeed pleased, Auntie, that you should be singing a holy hymn so early in the morning and while at your customary labors," said the minister.

"Yas, suh," replied the woman, "Dat's mah aig song."

"Your what?" he asked.

"Mah aig song," she answered. "Ah allers sings dat when Ah's boilin' aigs—two verses fuh sof'-boiled an' three verses fuh hah'd-boiled."

Mandy:—"Rastus, does yo' love me?"

Rastus:—"Yo's one gal Ah don't like none 'tuther bettah than!"   ,

AN UNKNOWN CHOICE

Isom was a stranger in the community. The night following his arrival in the city, a store was burglarized. Early the next morning, Isom was placed in jail and accused of the offense. A few days later he was arraigned for trial. Since the Negro was destitute and unknown, it became necessary for the court to appoint an attorney to represent him at the trial.

"Isom," said the judge, "I will give you the choice of selecting either of these attorneys. Of course, you do not know them, but each says he is a good lawyer. There's Mr. Green sitting on the right, and there's Mr. Jordan in front of you. Mr. Jones is down stairs. You can take your choice."

After observing critically each of the two attorneys present, Isom said:

"Jedge, please ast de two gemmen jes' tuh step outen de co't room while Ah tells yo' dat Ah choose de gemman down stairs dat Ah ain't nevah seen."

He:—"Honey-lam', is dat lovelight whut Ah sees shinin' in yo' eyes?"

She:—"Niggah, dat ain't lovelight—dat's mah stoplight."

A Shining Light

An old darkey was employed as a night
watchman at a railroad crossing in the suburbs of an Alabama city. It was his duty to
wave his red lantern and prevent the crossing of traffic while the cars were passing.

But one dark night the cars bumped into
a farmer, bruising him up, killing his team,
and smashing his wagon. The farmer
brought suit against the Railway Company
for damages. In the trial, the chief witness
for the Company was the Negro watchman,
the Railway resting its claim on the waving

of the lantern by the Negro. As a result of
his seemingly certain testimony that he
waved the lantern and that the farmer attempted to cross in spite of it, the jury found
a verdict in favor of the Railway Company.

That night the superintendent saw the old
Negro and expressed his thanks for the
money he had saved the Company. "You
certainly made a good witness," he said. "Did
you get scared?"

"Yas, suh," said the darkey, "Ah wuz suttinly skeered dat dey wuz goin' tuh ast me
ef dat lamp had a light in hit."

A REWARD FOR SILENCE

A colored minister became involved in an
affair which necessitated his resignation as
the spiritual leader of the flock. After ma-
ture deliberation, he concluded that he would
seek work among strangers in a distant and
unknown field.

The congregation assembled to hear the
sample sermon of the new minister and to
decide if the call should be made permanent.
As the minister arose, to his amazement he
recognized one of his old brethren seated in
the rear of the church. With calmness and
confidence he focused his eyes intently upon
his old friend and began as follows:

"Ah takes fuh mah text dis mawnin' dese wuhds ob de Apostle Paul which reads, *Dem dat sees me, an' knows me, an' sez nuthin', here or hereaftah, dem will Ah reward latah.*"

BETTER OR WORSE

The minister of a white church performed the ceremony which united Ezra and his dominating sweetheart in the bonds of matrimony. About six months later, Ezra returned to the minister and applied for a divorce.

"I can perform marriages, but I cannot dissolve them," said the preacher. "Besides, I do not think you should ask for a divorce, because you made a solemn promise that you would take your wife for better or for worse."

To this plea Ezra heatedly replied:

"Yas, suh, pahson, Ah knows dat, but she's wussen Ah tuk her fuh."

Sambo:—"Ah wants a razzoo."

Clerk:—"Safety razor?"

Sambo:—"No, suh, Ah wants hit fo' social puhposes!"

LOOKING WELL

An old time darkey, wearing an expression of anxiety upon his face, forced his way through the crowds of a department store.

"Fuh de goodness sake," he said, "Ah jes' simply cain't fin' nuthin' in dis stoh' atall."

"Are you looking for something in men's clothes?" inquired the polite floor-walker.

"Nossuh, boss, Ah ain't," explained the old Negro. "Ah's lookin' fuh sumpin' in wimmen's close—Ah's lost mah wife somewhar in dis stoh'."

LESSON IN LOGIC

Jeb Johnson had loaned a dollar to Si Simpkins, a shiftless Negro of his acquaintance. He had made many unsuccessful attemps to collect it. The provocation of Jeb and the shiftlessness of Si were made evident by the following argument:

Jeb: "Ah wants tuh know is yo' gwine'r pay me dat dollah. Is yo'?"

Si: "Ah ain't sayin' Ah ain't."

Jeb: "Ah ain't askin' yo' is yo' ain't; Ah's askin' yo' ain't yo' is."

Si: "Yeh, Ah's gwine'r pay hit ef Ah evah ketches yo' by yo'sef an' ain't nobody else aroun'."

Jeb: "But Ah's by mah se'f now. Den pay me right now."

Si: "No, yo' ain't. Ah's wid yo' now."

Unanswerable Logic

A fat travelling man stopped off between trains to call on his customers in a small town. He completed his work just in time to catch a noon train. It was a hot day, and he could find no conveyance of any kind to the station, which was located a mile and a half from town. Therefore, it was necessary to take his traveling bags in hand and to trudge on foot over a dusty road to the station.

With perspiration dripping from his forehead and with complete physical exhaustion, he staggered up to the little station just before the train arrived. No one was in sight except an old darkey who leaned lazily against the platform.

"Uncle," he inquired, "why in the world did they build this station so far from the town?"

"Ah don't know, boss," he said, "but Ah 'spose hit wuz 'case dey wanted tuh git hit closer tuh de railroad!"

More Mathematics

Two young colored men, dressed fastidiously in the brightest colors, were walking leisurely down the street. Their pompous appearance suggested rivalry in the art of making a profound impression upon the fair sex of the community. They evidently excelled in petting, prating, and pretending.

"Black boy, whut kin' ob seegar is dat yo' am smokin'?" asked the one.

"Niggah, dat's a quatah seegar!" came the answer.

"Quatah, nuthin', yo' lyin' jelly bean. Yo' nevah paid no two bits fuh no seegar."

"Ah didn't say nuthin' 'bout payin' nuthin' fuh nuthin'. De boss he smokes three quatahs, an' Ah smokes one quatah!"

DISCRIMINATING JUDGMENT

Sam and Jerry, two young men who vied with each other for social prominence in the colored community, were engaged in earnest conversation. Just then a black fly buzzed about Sam's head.

"Jerry, whut kind ob a fly am dis?"

"Dat am a hoss fly," replied Sambo.

"Whut am a hoss fly, Sambo?"

"A hoss fly?" queried Sam with a derisive look. "A hoss fly am a fly whut buzzes 'roun' an' 'roun' hosses an' jackasses. See him? Dar he come again!"

"Look heah, Niggah, yo' ain't callin' me no jackass, is yo'?"

"Ah ain't callin' yo' no jackass," answered Sam with still greater sarcasm, "But yo' cain't fool no hoss fly."

THE BLESSED TRINITY

A Negro preacher walked into the newspaper office of a small town and requested a business interview with the editor.

"Mistah Edito'," said the minister, "dey is forty-seben membahs ob mah chu'ch which subscribes fuh yo' papah. Do dat entitle me tuh hab a chu'ch notice in de papah?"

The editor assured him that he would be glad to run the announcement, and requested him to say what he wanted inserted. Whereupon, the minister dictated the following:

"Mount Hebron Babtis' Chu'ch—Reverend Josephus Hunnicutt, Pastah—Preachin', mawnin' an' night—In de promulgation ob de gospil, three books is necessary: De Bible, de hymn book, an' de pocketbook— Come an' bring all three."

A FORGIVING SPIRIT

"Mose," said the employer, "I am very sorry to learn that you buried your wife last week."

"Yassuh, boss, Ah jes' had to do dat— she wuz daid," answered the Negro. "Mistah, would yo' please lemme off agin next Sat'day?"

"Why do you want another day off so soon?"

"Well, suh, yo' see—so Ah kin' git married agin."

"Married! How can you think of treating your dead wife with such little consideration by marrying again so soon!"

"Well, suh, boss," answered the widower forgivingly, "Ah doesn't hol' no grudge agin' no one puhson very long."

DO EXPLANATIONS EXPLAIN?

Rastus was caught loafing in the vicinity of a farmer's hen house. The farmer immediately counted his chickens and discovered that several were missing. Whereupon, he accused Rastus of stealing them.

The Negro stoutly denied any connection with the theft. In fact, he volunteered his services to help find the culprit. Disgusted at the darkey's tactics, the farmer gave the Negro a lecture on courtesy.

"Rastus, when you talk to me hereafter, I want you to be as polite as you know how." Then he demanded that the Negro take off his hat. As he removed it, a chicken flew out. Very quickly and quite convincingly, Rastus exclaimed:

"Well, Ah'll be doggone ef dat pesky pullet ain't went an' crawled up mah pant leg an' up tuh mah haid!"

WILLING TEAM WORK

An old Negro was resting his yoke of oxen under the shade of a tree on a hot summer day, while he dozed on the wagon. A white man came along and engaged him in conversation about his oxen.

"That's a fine yoke of oxen, Uncle," said the white man. "What are their names?"

"Dat's Buck ovah dar, an' dis is Tobe ovah heah," came the reply.

"You say they are a willing team—which is the more willing of the two?" he was asked.

"Well, suh, dey is bof willin' 'bout de same," answered the darkey.

"That is unusual," said the white man. "You say one is about as willing as the other?"

"Yas, suh, near ez Ah kin tell," chuckled the Negro. "Buck ovah dar am willin' tuh pull de whole wagen an' load, an' Tobe ovah heah am puffeckly willin' tuh let 'im do hit."

THE SCARCITY OF TEETH

The minister waxed eloquent and held his audience spellbound as he preached on the awful horrors of hell. As he clinched each point, there resounded from the front seats choruses of "Amen! Bruddah, dat sho' am de truf, amen!" When he finished the phrase, "an' Ah tells yo', mah Bredren, dere will be weepin' and wailin' an' gnashin' ob teeth," there was a sudden burst of emotion in the front pew.

"Whut's de mattah wid yo', Sistah Myriah?" he asked.

"Ah ain't got no teeth! Ah ain't got no teeth!" answered Myriah triumphantly.

"Dat don't make no diffe'nce, Sistah Myriah, de teeth will be fuhnished," said the preacher.

THE DOCTOR FORGOT

The patient was sick, and the longer he was attended by the Negro doctor, the sicker he became. When he was discharged and a white doctor was summoned, the latter encountered much difficulty in ascertaining the course of treatment administered by his predecessor.

"Now, tell me," said the white doctor, "exactly what the Negro doctor did. Did he take your temperature?"

With a disgusted expression, the sick patient answered:

"Nossuh, Ah don't reckin' he did. Ah ain't missed nuthin' but mah watch yit."

UNITED BROTHERHOOD

A well-known character around a small town was Uncle Jeb who lived by the charity of church people. Uncle Jeb's agreeable diplomacy was well illustrated by this incident:

One day as he was passing down the street, dressed in a suit of many colors and many pieces, he was asked what church he had become affiliated with in order to procure such fine clothes.

"Well," said Uncle Jeb, "de shoes wuz gib tuh me by de Babtis', de hat by de Meffedis, de britches by de Presbyterens, de coat by de Luthrens, de ves' by de Cath'lics, de shirt by de Deciples, an' de red neck tie by de 'Piscopalians. Ah 'spose, under dese circumstances, dat Ah mus' b'long tuh de United Bredren."

RETURNED MERCHANDISE

A muscular darkey consulted a local doctor about his health. The doctor's careful examination revealed that there was no chronic disorder and that the patient's trouble was due chiefly to overeating. As a consequence, the prescribed menu excluded, for a few weeks only, all kinds of meat. Fried chicken was, of course, prohibited.

As the Negro was leaving, the doctor called him back and said: "You've forgotten something, haven't you? My fee for the advice I have given you is four dollars."

"Yeh," answered the darkey as he resumed his leave, "but Ah is returnin' yo' advice an' ain't gwine'r take hit; so Ah doesn't owe yo' nuthin', doctah."

INTEREST IS INTERESTING

George had made a loan of three dollars to one of his colored friends. When the debt came due he was unable to collect it. He dunned him many times, obtaining neither money nor encouragement. After much delay, the friend positively refused to pay and even denied the obligation. In his distress, George finally decided to consult a lawyer for advice.

"What reason does he give for refusing to pay the debt?" asked the lawyer.

"Boss," said the darkey, "he say he done owed me dat money fo' so long dat de int'-rust had et it all up, an' now he don't owe me nuthin'."

THE CALL OF HEAVEN

A large company of the descendants of
Ham had assembled in a dark room to witness communications with departed spirits
through the medium of a strange, mysteri-
ous Negro who was said to possess this su-
pernatural power. It was agreed by those
present that communication should be established with Sam and Jezra, two well-
known characters who had died three
months previous in the same explosion at
the munitions plant.

The mediator succeeded immediately in

establishing direct and uninterrupted communication with each of the departed brothers. It was found that Jezra had gone to the celestial kingdom above while Sam had been cast into utter darkness in the lower regions where there was weeping and wailing and gnashing of teeth.

"Whut yo' doin' down here, Sam, an' how is yo' gittin' 'long?" they inquired. 'Gittin' 'long fine," came the prompt reply. "De Debil he got us all dressed up in big red robes wid long ho'ns, an' us has to shovel coal sometimes. But de Debil he ain't heah much, so us gits jes' lots ob res'. All de boys am havin' mouty good times."

Then they made inquiry of Jezra as to his welfare. "Oh, ain't gittin' 'long so well —so much wuhk tuh do dat hit am ruinatious. Yo' know us has tuh git up at fo' 'clock in de mawnin', go out an' sweep de clouds, polish de stahs, gather in de moon, hang out de sun! Hit sho' am mos' awful —so much wuhk! But de trouble am dat us is mouty shawt on he'p up heah."

Judge:—"Liza, you've been brought in for intoxication."

Liza:—"Dat's good. Boss, yo' kin stahrt right now, please!"

HELP NEEDED

In the course of his sermon, a Negro minister observed the presence of a new face in his congregation. When the service was ended, he hurried down to greet and welcome the newcomer.

"Bruddah Mosely, Ah has knowed yo' fuh ten yeahs an' dis am de fus' time Ah's r'cognized yo' face in dis chu'ch. Yo' sho' does need tuh come some mo' ef yo' specks tuh git tuh Hebben."

Whereupon Mosely said: "Yo' sho' am right, Pahson. Ah jes' had tuh come. Ah needs some strengthin'. Ah's got a job nex' week white-washin' a chicken coop an' buildin' a fence 'roun' a watah melon patch."

HAPPY DAY

Mandy was madly in love with Jethro, despite the latter's lack of enthusiasm and his constitutional aversion to all forms of labor. Her love had gone beyond the point of blindness and had reached the stage of deafness, dumbness, and insanity. Financial embarrassment was the barrier to the consummation of her plans.

"When is yo' an' dat Jethro gwine'r git married an' quit so much ob dis high-tone lovin' an' thinkin' so much ob one anudder?" inquired one of her friends.

"Well, 'tain't gwine'r be long," answered

Mandy. "All Ah's gotta do now is tuh buy a white trusso, an' rent a house, an' buy Jethro a suit ob close, an' git 'im a job, an' fin' some reg'lar washin' fo' mahself. An' when dem's done, Ah kin name de happy day!"

THE ART OF FORGETTING

Uncle Ned was a good old darkey who was responsible, who possessed an abundance of common sense, and who had great originality in expressing philosophical truths in terse phrases.

"Why is it, Uncle," asked a white friend, "that we read every day of white people committing suicide, but we never hear of a darkey ending his life in that way?"

"Well, suh, boss, hit am lak dis: When a white puhson have troubles, he sets down an' gits a studyin' an' a worryin' an' a worryin' 'till he cain't stan' hit no longah. Den de fus thing yo' knows sumpin' goes 'bang!'—he's done killed hisse'f."

"But when a Niggah sets down an' stahts a worryin' 'bout his troubles, he jes' natch'ly falls off tuh sleep an' fuhgets tuh do hit 'till hit's too late."

Smart Ancestors

Mose Tucker, an extremely courteous darkey, was very talkative. He possessed great egotism, and was particularly proud of his family connections.

"Lemme tell yo'," said Mose as he spoke reverently in memory of his father who had passed many years before to his eternal reward, "dat man sho' wuz smaht. Ah's know'd lots ob smaht men, but dat ole man ob mine wuz de smahtest man whut Ah evah did see in all my bo'n days. He wuz so smaht dat he fo'tole de very day an' hour an' minit dat he wuz gonna die. Wuzent dat smaht?"

"How did he do this so accurately?" asked his white listener.

"Well——er——De sheriff tole 'im," said Mose.

Moving Heaven and Earth

An old-time Negro revival was in progress in a rural community of a Southern state. Near the place of meeting was a well of cool water, generously supplied from a spring on the side of the mountain above. It was only five feet to the top of the water which stood twice that depth in the bottom of the well. Over the well was a square box, opened at the top and at the bottom.

The services were long and the physical exertion of the participants great, necessitating frequent trips to the well for water. Some mischievous white boys slipped to the well during the services one evening and moved the box a few feet away from its proper place.

About eleven o'clock a fat and perspiring Negro woman walked briskly toward the well to quench her excessive thirst. Suddenly she stepped into the well, was completely submerged beneath the water, then rose to the surface crying out in desperation:

"Oh mah Lawd! Oh mah Lawd! Some fool sinnah done gone an' moved dat well!"

A GOOD PROVIDER

Mandy and her husband had encountered much domestic infelicity during the last few years. When Mandy applied for a position as cook, she was asked if her husband was a good provider for her and the family.

"He jes' ain't nuthin' else but," answered the Negro woman. "He's always providin' an' don't do nuthin' else. He gwine'r git some new fuhniture, providin' he git de money; he gwine'r git de money, providin' he go to wuhk; he gwine'r go to wuhk, providin' de job suit 'im. Ah nevah has seed sech a providin' Niggah in all mah bo'n days!"

Business Insight

A portly Negro woman entered the door of the office and inquired if she could get a fire insurance policy on her husband.

"This is the fire insurance office, but what you want is life insurance, not fire insurance," said the clerk.

"Nossuh," she replied, "Ah doesn't. Whut Ah craves an' whut Ah's gwine'r git is fire inshorance, 'case dat triflin' Niggah's been fired fo' times in de las' seben days."

An Erring Urchin

Rube Stephens, a colored youth, was arraigned before a magistrate on a charge of stealing chickens at two o'clock in the morning from a friendly neighbor. Despite his protests of innocence, the evidence pointed conclusively to the defendant's guilt.

"This man says he saw you at two o'clock in the morning," said the judge, "and that when he fired the first shot he saw you run from his chicken coop. How do you explain this, Rube?"

"He could easy be mistaken, Jedge," answered the confused Negro. "In de fust place, hit wuzent me he seen. In de secon'

place, dahk as de night wuz an' fas' as Ah
wuz running', hit could a been anudder Niggah whut faintly resembles me!"

No Samples

Jake, porter at the small-town hotel, knew
intimately all the old traveling salesmen.
But a new salesman arrived on the scene,
and Jake lost no opportunity to find out all
about him. The porter made inquiry as to
the whereabouts of his trunks but was informed that he carried no excess baggage
of that kind.

"You see," said the salesman, "I sell intelligence, and it is unnecessary for me to have
trunks."

"Well," answered the Negro, "yo' am de
fus' travelin' man Ah evah seen who ain't
carryin' no samples."

Devoid of Understanding

Rufus had been the husband of Dinah for
many years. It had taken a wise expendi-
ture of his meager wages to meet the de-
mands of an exacting wife. Among the
things that Dinah had admired was a beautiful skunk wrap. With the practice of econ-

omy, Rufus was finally able to purchase the coveted article.

"Well, Dinah, how much does yo' admire it?" asked Rufus.

"It sho' am a convalescin' wrap," said Dinah. "But dey is one thing Ah cain't figger out; an' dat am how dis mos' fines' fur kin come fum sech a lowdown, stinkin' animule!"

With a broken heart and in utter despair, Rufus answered.

"Ah doesn't see how yo' kin call me sech mean names as dat!"

Spilling the Beans

A colored workman had been indicted and placed on trial for stealing a watch. In the trial he exercised the prerogative of a defendant in refusing to give testimony in the case. The evidence was rather vague and somewhat contradictory, as a consequence of which the judge dismissed the case.

"The defendant is discharged," ordered the judge.

Since he was not conversant with court procedure, the Negro stood dazed at the abrupt ending and was reluctant to assume his freedom.

"You are discharged. You may go," repeated the judge.

Whereupon the Negro answered in a confidential tone:

"Jedge, does dat mean Ah has tuh gib de watch back?"

IN CASE OF AN ACCIDENT

During the World War when men were being drafted for military service, there appeared before one of the local boards a burly black from the Brazos river bottoms of Texas. Because of his unshapely feet, brought about by going bare-footed since childhood, the board decided that it was economy to exempt him rather than to bear the expense of providing handmade shoes.

But the feeling against slackers was so strong that the Negro insisted that he be accepted for some kind of service. He was sent to the munitions plant where a series of questions was propounded before he would be permitted to go to work.

"This is very dangerous work and men are being killed by explosions every day," they told him. "Where do you want the remains sent in the event of a serious accident?"

"How is dat, Boss, whar do yo' want de which sent?" the Negro asked.

"Where do you want the remains sent?" they repeated.

Reaching for his hat, with the whites of his eyes protruding, he said:

"Boss, ef hits jes' de same tuh yo', Ah'll take 'em wid me right now."

THE TAINT OF TEMPTATION

In a certain city of Oklahoma, a young Negress, scantily clad, was brought before the municipal court, charged with drunkenness and disorderly conduct. When the judge observed the absence of proper attire, he suggested that she go home and put on additional clothing.

"Jedge," she answered impudently, "Ah 'spects Ah kin dress mah body lak Ah wants to!"

"You are fined five dollars for contempt of this court," retorted the magistrate.

When she went to the desk of the clerk, she was asked what the fine was for. In a haughty manner and a rebuking voice, the young Negress replied:

"De jedge say dat Ah is fined five dollahs fuh temptin' de cote!!"

THE CONVENIENCE OF INCONVENIENCE

Henry Webster was mowing the lawn with unusual leisure. He would push the dilapidated mower for a few seconds, then sit down for several minutes to repair it.

"How much do you get for mowing lawns?" inquired a white man who had observed the slow procedure.

"Thirty cents a houhr," answered Henry proudly.

"Why don't you dispose of the old mower and buy a good one?"

"Wharfo' does Ah need a bettah one dan

Ah is now got, Mistah Butlah?" asked the darkey with a look of surprise.

"Because you could do twice as much work in half the time."

"Yeah," responded the Negro, "but Ah ain't got twice ez much wuhk tuh do, an' Ah is gittin' in all de time dey is!"

LOADED WITH DYNAMITE

George Abraham Washington had a natural antipathy for work. Consequently, he was gratified when the doctor prescribed the rest cure.

"Your salivary glands are swollen and you have a torpid liver," said the doctor. "You must be quiet, or serious consequences will ensue."

George was proud of his ailments, and he took every opportunity to advertise them. Besides, it gave him a good alibi when his wife threatened to strike him with the poker because of failure to work.

"Pacify yo'se'f, Mandy, an' don't touch me wid dat poker," he said proudly. "Ah is a sick man, an' de doctah done tole me dat mah salvation glands is swelled, an' Ah's got a torpedo on my livah, an' Ah's li'ble tuh blow up any minit!"

THE FIRST RADIO

The Negro preacher grew eloquent as he explained the difficult portions of the Bible to his flock.

Finally he announced to his congregation that there was nothing new in the world, that the Bible mentioned all things that they had ever seen or heard about. Then one doubtful brother challenged the preacher to find anything about the radio in the Scriptures.

"Dat am de easiest topic ob all," said the minister. "Fuh de Good Book say dat, in de beginnin', dat po' ole Adam were a mouty lonesome man. He didn't hab nobody tuh talk tuh 'im. Den de Lawd sent 'im a loud speakah, an' hit been broadcastin' evah since! Ast me sumptin' mo', bred'ren."

MONEY TALKS

The Negro church had a large attendance, but its interests were suffering by the failure of its members to pay their dues. As a result, the minister and deacon Burns determined upon drastic action for the following Sunday.

"We has a collection tuh make dis mawnin' fuh de sake ob yo' pussonal repuions," dolefully announced the preacher to his flock. "We is now goin' tuh pass de plate, an' whichevah ob yo' has stole Mistah Riley's tuhrkeys, don't put nuthin' on de plate."

"Listen," interposed Deacon Burns, "evah blessed Niggah in de chu'ch dat ain't stole no tuhrkeys, come down wid de rocks."

The collection was successful.

LYING CRUSHED TO EARTH

As usual, the darkies had assembled on the steps of Deacon Jim's store to exchange stories and pleasantries of the community. Rastus was the center of attraction as he spoke of his personal achievements.

"Folks, yo' notice Ah wuzent heah las' Sunday, 'cause Ah wuz callin' on mah gal.

"We stahted out ridin' wid a team ob mules.

"B'fo' we know'd hit we wuz drivin' a col' black hawse hitched tuh a fine red buggy.

"All ob a sudden we found ouhrselves in a Chev'let coupe, jus' a sailin' down de boulevahd!

"Den we realize we wuz a whizzin' th'u de air in a air plane, goin' ninety miles a houhr!!

"Right sudden we done busted into a cloud, an' when Ah woke up dar wuz a wing lyin'

undah de tree, an' dar wuz de propellah lyin'
ovah de do', an' dar wuz a wheel lyin' by
de plane, an' dar wuz de gal lyin' on de
groun'!!!"

"But whar wuz yo' a lyin', Rastus?" asked
one of the leaders.

"Oh me? W'y Ah wuz jus' a lyin' all de
time!" answered Rastus.

TALKING WITH JEHOVAH

Efe Adams, despite his protests of innocence, was sentenced by the judge to a long
term of imprisonment at hard labor. The
sheriff was leading the sentenced man away
when the judge, his face aflame with indig-
nation, ordered the prisoner brought back to
the bar.

"What do you mean by using profane
language in connection with this court? How
dare you curse me? I am strongly tempted
to add five years to your sentence."

"Jedge, Ah didn't say nuthin' agin yo',"
answered the Negro.

"Do you mean to tell me that a minute
ago, as you were being led away, you did not
mutter profane utterances aimed at the dignity of this court?"

"No, suh, jedge, lemme tell yo', please,
suh," answered the Negro penitently. "Ah

was jest thinkin' dat eben ef Ah can't get no justice in dis wurld, Ah shorely will be able to 'splain dis mess when Ah gits tuh Hebben. So Ah begin talkin' tuh mahse'f an' sez: 'God am de jedge! God am de jedge'— jes' lak dat ."

M. D. AND H. D. PRESCRIPTIONS

Abraham Johnson, a Negro farmer, was ill. The medical doctor prescribed. It so happened that Abe's old gray horse, taking advantage of his owner's illness, developed a severe case of colic as a result of grazing in a patch of green cane. Then the horse doctor prescribed.

Whereupon, it was decided that the Negro's wife should go to the village to obtain the necessary medicines for both patients. The druggist told the woman to come for the medicines in a few minutes. When she returned, she spoke earnestly as follows:

"Be mouty keerful tuh write plain on de bottles which is fuh de hawse an' which is fuh Abe. Ah doesn't want nuthin' tuh happen tuh dat hawse b'fo' de spring plowin' is done!"

Rescue the Dying

Elisha Snow, whose life had been filled
with many intentional mistakes, was told by
the minister that he was about to die. The
preacher was making haste to complete his
work before the end.

"Bruddah Snow," he said, "yo' musn't die
hatin' nobody. Ef Mose Johnson done yo'
wrong, yo' mus' furgit hit."

"Ah does furgit, Bruddah, but Ah's got 'er
pow'ful bad mem'ry, an' Ah keeps furgittin'
dat Ah furgot!" answered the penitent.

"But yo' mus' furgive 'im b'fo' yo' dies,
Bruddah Snow. Jus' say right now dat yo'
furgives 'im."

"Den Ah does furgive Mose Johnson ef Ah
doesn't git well, Pahson. But ef Ah gits
well, dat damn Niggah bettah hotfoot hit
clean out'en dis country!"

Origin of the Species

A young white woman, taking compassion
upon a group of back-yard pickaninnies,
who lacked opportunities, announced that
she would organize a Sunday school for the
purpose of teaching them some of the sim-
pler truths of the Bible. On the first Sunday
morning, ten enthusiastic disciples appeared

and sat under the shade of a large oak tree.

"Who made you?" she asked the first boy. Then she taught him to answer, "God made me."

"What did God make you out of?" she asked the second boy. Then she taught him to answer, "He made me out of dirt."

Each child was asked a question and taught the answer to it. When she had given each pupil the answer to a question, the teacher decided she would test them upon the lessons taught.

Returning to the first child, she asked, "Who made you?"

"Dirt!" came the quick answer.

"Why, no!" said the teacher, "didn't I tell you that God made you?"

"No mam, Miss Lucy, hit wuzn't me Gawd made," retorted the little Negro. "Dat black boy whut Gawd made sneaked 'round de corner ob de house when yo' wuzn't lookin'."

Multum in Parvo

The gaunt figure of Iscariot Jones stood before the judge, charged with stealing a fat pullet from Aunt Malindy Moses, the prosecuting witness.

"Iscariot Jones," asked the judge sternly,

"did you steal that pullet from Aunt Malindy as charged?"

"No suh," answered the defendant, "takin' whut has already been stole ain't stealin', jedge."

"Then did you take the pullet from Aunt Malindy?"

"Jedge, Ah jus' tuck hit fuh a lit'l joke."

"How far did you carry it?"

" 'Bout fo'teen blocks fum whar Aunt Malindy lives tuh whar Ah is temporar'ly residin'."

"Ten days," sighed the Judge. "That was carrying a little joke too far!"

A Slight Error

Mandy Malone, a corpulent woman, was a material witness in a trial at court. In the course of the trial, the age of the Negro woman became an important fact in the case. Whereupon, the judge propounded the following questions:

"How old are you, Mandy?"

"Ah is seventy-three jedge," came the answer.

"Are you sure?"

"Yassuh, co'se Ah is."

"Mandy, you don't look to be seventy-three."

"Ah shuah is, jedge, or Ah wouldn't said hit."

After a few minutes the trial was interrupted by Mandy.

"Jedge, please suh, 'bout dat age. Ah furgits, ceptin' Ah knows now hit ain't no seventy-three; dat's mah waist line."

LYING FOR TRUTH

A Negro youth had been indicted for violating the laws of the commonwealth. When he came to trial, he plead that he was not guilty of the charge.

His attorney, a young lawyer who was trying his first case, insisted that he prove an alibi. After much argument, in the private conversation that preceded, the Negro reluctantly agreed to take the advice of his counsel. When informed of the defendant's plea, the court said:

"Does the defendant understand what an alibi is?"

"Yassuh," answered the Negro, "Ah knows all 'bout hit. Dat's provin' dat yo' wuz at de pray'r-meetin' whar yo' wuzent, in ordah tuh show tuh de ign'rance ob de co'te dat yo' wuzent at de crap-game whar' yo' wuz!"

THE AGE OF UNREASON

On the second morning after the Negro cook began her work for a white family, she brought her five-year old son. The boy's conduct soon provoked the mother, and she reprimanded the youth severely.

"Fertilizer! Fertilizer! Take yo' black fingers outen dat cake dough! Fertilizer, git outen dat kitchen, b'fo' Ah busts yo' hahd haid wide open!"

These words were observed by the lady who calmly inquired the reason for calling the boy Fertilizer.

"Dat's his name," answered the servant.

"Why did you give him such a peculiar name?"

"He wuz so wuthless," answered the Negro, "we didn't want no mo' chilluns. So we named him fuh bof ob us—Ferdinand fuh his Pa and Eliza fuh his Ma. Don't dat spell Ferd-Eliza?"

NO TIME FOR PRAYER

The minister discoursed long and eloquently upon the importance of right living. Especially did he urge the observance of the commandment not to steal, to all of which the members gave hearty approval.

Two members, one a deacon, were unable

to resist the temptation to enter a chicken house, by the roadside, as they returned home after the services.

"Bruddah," observed the Negro on the inside of the house, "Ah wuz jus' thinkin' how wicked we is, goin' tuh chu'ch on Sunday night, hearin' 'er pow'ful sermon, prayin' lak we did, den stealin' dese chickens b'fo' we gits home."

"Dis ain't no time fuh argufyin' an' prayin'," ejaculated the deacon. "Dat am 'er moral question, an' we can sputify on dat nex' Sunday night. Han' me down anuddah pullet, Bruddah Simpson."

Politics and Theology

The minister was conducting an examination to ascertain if Magnesia Mills was qualified to be received into the church as a candidate for baptism.

"Ain't yo' nevah stole nuthin'?" asked the preacher.

"Nevah, bruddah, nevah, in mah whole life," answered the candidate with emphasis.

"Never stole er chicken?"

"Not eben er little chicken, bruddah."

"Nevah tuck er watah milyun?"

"Not eben got in er watah milyun patch aftah dahk, bruddah."

"Didn't yo' nevah take er hawg when yo' wuz hungry?"

"Not eben er ham, Pahrson."

"Look heah, yo' lyin' rascal," said the minister, "yo' comes up heah tuh jine de chu'ch an' won't eben confess yo' black sins. Hotfoot yo'se'f outen dis sacred temple. Dis ain't no political pahty, dis am er chu'ch!"

A CONDITIONAL PRAYER

The story is told that Andrew Carnegie, while on a vacation in the South, visited a modest Negro church for the Sunday morning services. He came unannounced and he was entirely unknown to the congregation.

At the proper time one patriarchal-appearing deacon passed the plate for collection. The members contributed meager sums, the total amounting to one dollar and twenty-nine cents. Imagine the surprise when Carnegie threw in a fifty-dollar bill. With bulging eyes and with silent glee, the deacon reported the large contribution to the pastor. Then the pastor fervently rendered thanks as follows:

"Oh, Lawd, bless dis large congregation and dis small contribution whut dey has give. An', oh Lawd, 'spesh'ly bless dis welcome vis'tur an' de large contribution whut he 'pears tuh have made; providin', Oh Lawd, dat dis fifty-dollah bill am Simon pure money an' genuine, an' ain't no counterfeit!"

FACTS SPEAK FOR THEMSELVES

On the farms of the Brazos River in Texas, there lived a group of successful Negro farmers. Among them was Uncle Ezra who was a sage among the people of his race and to whom other Negroes carried their troubles.

One morning Aunt Saphronia, a widow in the community, appeared to get advice about her pigs.

"Ah tells yo', Uncle Ezra," she said, "sumptin' is mouty wrong wid dem pigs. Evah mawnin' Ah finds three or fo' lyin' in de lot, col' an' stiff, wid de feet in de air. Ah wants tuh know, whut am de mattah wid dem pigs?"

Uncle Ezra scratched his head and then said calmly:

"Looks tuh me lak yo' pigs is daid!"

A STITCH IN TIME

A Southern white woman stopped an old Negro on the street and extended smypathy for his recent misfortune.

"Mose," she said, "I'm certainly sorry that Aunt Lucy has left you so suddenly."

"Yassum, she done got 'er divo'ce an' gone back tuh Alabam," answered the Negro with a grin.

"Besides the inconvenience to you, Mose, I am certainly worried about who is going to do my washing now. Aunt Lucy has been with me so long."

"Don't yo' fret, Missus," answered the Negro. "Dis depression ain't gona las' long. Ah's co'tin' again' an' when Ah co'tes, Ah sho' do co'te fast."

White Friend:—"Does that mule ever kick you, Sam?"

Sam:—"No suh, but sometime he kick whar Ah is jes' been!"

THE DEVIL DIDN'T

A Negro of formidable appearance was being tried on a charge of brutality. The mutilated person was brought into court. The face of the victim was merely a recent site where a face had been.

After the jury had returned a verdict of guilty, the Judge said:

"This is the worst case of brutality I have ever seen. A human being would have to be under the influence of the devil to wreck so completely the countenance of a fellow creature. Both demons and the devil must have urged you on."

"Jedge," said the prisoner, "hit do look lak yo' is right. Hit do seem lak tuh me when Ah wuz separatin' his nose fum his face wid a razo' de debil wuz right behind me; an' Ah' spects hit wuz de demons whut tole me tuh stomp his front teeth out; but jedge, bitin' off his ear—dat wuz strictly mah own ideer."

BAD ACOUSTICS

The grand jury was in session, making close investigation of all violations of the law. At the same time the fervent preaching of the Reverend Joshua Phillips brought conviction to the wrong doers of the colored congregation. The penitent deacon wavered between contradictory emotions. Finally, he could stand it no longer.

"Bruddahs," he shouted, "Ah throws mahse'f in de ahms ob de Lawd, an' Ah wants yo' all tuh know whut a pore an' wretched sinner Ah has been. But bruddahs, Ah mus' pacify mahse'f while de gran' jury am meetin'."

"Come on, deacon," retorted the minister, "confess yo' unholy sins tuh yo' Redeemah now! De Lawd wants tuh fo'gib yo'."

"Yeah, Ah knows dat, preacher. He'll fo'gib me right now; but de Lawd, he ain't sittin' on dat gran' jury!"

UNSPEAKABLE EVIDENCE

Miss Lucretia Longbottom, a colored belle of Shreveport, received company regularly from Mr. Boots Arrington, one of the leaders in finance among the Negroes of the city. At first, the wooing of Boots was ardent and persistent; then his calls were less frequent; and finally, his attentions were discontinued altogether.

One morning Lucretia blew into the office of a Negro attorney. Her broken heart had given way to an expression of determined retaliation.

"Ah wants tuh sue dat Boots Arrington fuh breach ob promises, an' Ah wants hit done widout prolongations," she said commandingly.

"Is yo' got de low-down evidence dat he made love tuh you?" asked the attorney.

"Is Ah? Ah ain't got nuthin' else but! Ah got fo' wore-out sofa pillows, one busted sofa, an' a lamp dat won't light!"

WHEN MAN FINDS HIMSELF

From the proceeds that came from a raid upon a neighbor's chicken house, Sam and Magnolia spent a wild night talking eloquently to the ebony bones while in a state of deep intoxication. The next day, they boasted of their pleasures to each other.

"How is yo' on de mawnin' aftah de night befo'?" queried Magnolia.

"Niggah," said Sam, "Ah sho' spent er mos' wil' night! Ah nevah in all mah unbo'n days seen so many lamp posts an' trees an' stahrs an' moons an' merry-go-roun's! Boy, mah haid wuz sho' exaggeratin' whut mah eyes didn't see! How'd yo' fin' yo'se'f, Magnoya?"

"How'd Ah fin' mahse'f!" ejaculated Magnolia. "Come mighty nigh nevah findin' mahse'f, Sambo. Yo' know whut? W'en Ah looked undah de table las' night, whut yo' reckon Ah seen? Nuthin'! Den, we'n Ah looked undah de table dis mawnin', whut yo' s'pose Ah seen! Boy w'en Ah looked undah de table dis mawnin', dar Ah wuz!"

SERENADING HIS SOUL

A white man was supervising several groups of Negroes who were working at manual labor. The work was hard and the sun was hot. When the boss made his periodical visit to one of the groups, about eleven o'clock a. m., he observed that one of the workmen was missing. Inquiry failed to locate him. "He jus' absconded hisse'f widout provaricatin' his where'bouts," said one of the others.

After a diligent search, the boss found the Negro about six hundred feet way, lying under the shade of a giant tree, his bony legs crossed and one foot dangling in the air as it kept time with the rhythmic strains of an old banjo which he lazily picked.

"Get up from there, you black scalawag! What do you mean by quitting your work like this right in the middle of the morning?" asked the impatient and irate foreman. The Negro arose, collected himself calmly, then answered in a piously courteous tone:

"Boss, Ah's been er wuhkin' Niggah all

mah bo'n days. Ah jus' wuhks an' wuhks
an' wuhks. Ah doesn't know nuthin' else
but wuhkin'. But sometimes, Boss, Ah jus'
has tuh git off clean by mahse'f an' serenade
mah soul!"

An Unseen Trouble

A United States Government official, in
one of the campaigns to stamp out hook-
worm, arrived in a town in Southern Mississippi. The visitor soon observed that Negroes and hound dogs constituted the greater
part of the population in the village.

As the official made his initial survey of
the situation, his attention was particularly
attracted to the pathetic wails of a long-
eared, unambitious hound dog that sat on his
hind quarters a few feet away.

"What is the matter with that dog?" the
visitor asked Uncle Ephriam who was passing by.

"He got de hook-worhm," replied the Negro.

"The hook-worm! Why the dog is in pain.
I thought the hookworm was painless and
made its victims sleepy and inactive."

"Yas, suh, hit do," replied the darkey.
"But yo' see dat dawg is settin' on a kuckle-
buhr an' is jes' too doggone lazy tuh git up
an' shake hisse'f!"

The Doctor's Prescription

Hal Ketchum was the proud owner of a mule team which he drove in hauling freight from the depot to an inland town about eight miles away. The mules were very amiable except at occasional times when they would together balk and refuse to pull. Such conduct always agitated Hal unduly, and the consequent beatings usually had the effect of making the animals more stubborn in their refusal to pull.

One day the mules balked on the road some four miles before they reached the end of their journey, refusing to move. About this time a country doctor, while passing on a professional call, stopped.

"I can make them go if you wish me to," said the doctor.

"Ef yo' kin, yo' am de hoss doctah Ah is cravin'," answered the indignant Negro.

The doctor removed from his case a hypodermic needle and quickly injected a small quantity of fluid into each animal. Immediately, the mules moved forward, tore themselves from the rickety wagon, and proceeded at break-neck speed down the road. As he saw the mules turn a curve in the road, almost out of sight, the darkey hastily rolled up one of his sleeves, rushed toward the doctor, and yelled at the top of his voice:

"Doc, gemme 'bout fo' times as much ob dat stuff whut yo' gib dem balky beasts, Ah got tuh ketch dem mules!"

BUSTED BLUNDERS

A colored brother experienced much difficulty in collecting dues to the fraternal order of which he was the Secretary-Treasurer. The negligent members were many, and they gave no heed whatever to the frequently occurring statements of the official that "dues is due."

Their failure to respond to these appeals weighed heavily upon the mind of the officer. Besides, he was sorely embarrassed at the depleted condition of the exchequer, which prevented the payment of his salary, and which brought constant embarrassment by the accumulation of unpaid bills. In a moment of desperation, he upbraided the unworthy members of the fraternity in a letter of scathing rebuke. The reproof was effective, and the money poured in. Some brought the money; others sent it. Among the latter was a communication which read as follows:

"Dear Brudder: Here am de five dollahs whut yo' sez Ah owes fuh dues. Please credit same tuh dis wayfarin' membah ob de great fraternity. But Ah mus' say, in de name ob justis an' truf', dat yo' made two awful mistakes in de good lettah whut yo' wrote: yo' spelt skunk wid a *c* an' lousy wid two *s's!* Yours in brudderly luv."

HUNGRY FOR WORK

Two Alabama Negroes started out from a small town to see the world. They were in a hilarious mood until their money ran out and they became stranded in a strange town. Hunger and the lack of friends forced them to seek employment. Jobs were scarce, and they became desperately hungry. Then one of the pair approached, with much humility, a passing white man.

"Mistah," he said, "Ah needs wuhk bad an' Ah suttinly hopes mebbe yo' kin he'p me out, please suh."

"You are very lucky," said the man. "I have just had a telephone call that the Eagle Laundry, down the street, is in need of a man. I would advise that you go down there immediately."

"Thank yo' mistah, thank yo'," said the Negro as he walked away. Then he stopped suddenly and said:

"Boss, mebbe dey'll use me; but Ah ain't neveh had no sperience washin' eagles."

More Evidence

When the fight between two colored boys had ended, it was discovered that no serious damage had been done except that one had severed the jugular vein of the other. As a result, the victor was brought before the magistrate and charges filed.

"Here you are again, Rube," said the magistrate. "Looks like your trouble gets worse every time. This is indeed a serious charge. Do you want me to appoint a lawyer to defend you?"

"No, suh, jedge," replied the youth solemnly. "Evah time de law gits me, Ah been gittin' a lawyah. Den dey slams me in de calaboose an' lets de lawyah go scott free. Jedge, ef hit's jus' de same wid yo' dis time, Ah's gwine'r throw mahse'f on de ig'rance ob de co'te."

———————

Elixcie:—"Castoria, whaffo' yo' goin' in dat beauty shop?"

Castoria:—"Big boy, Ah's goin' tuh git me a puhmanent straight!"

———————

Lieutenant:—"Do you want to take a ride in my airplane?"

Rastus:—"No, suh—I stays on terrah firmah, an' de mo' firmah, de less terrah!"

Matrimonial Economy

Minerva, the colored cook, announced to her mistress that she was going to be married.

"But I thought you were already married," said the mistress.

"Ah is," explained Minerva, "but seems lak mah ole man an' me is both done lost ouhr taste fuh one 'nother. 'Sides which, he's done got hisse'f ongaged tuh a yaller gal dat wuhks down tuh de terbaccer stemmery. So bein' him an' Gawge is good frien's, we is gona have'r double weddin' Tuesday night."

The woman told her that would never do as they could be prosecuted for bigamy. But Minerva said they could not afford a divorce which would cost sixteen dollars. Whereupon, the white woman gave her the necessary money.

On the following Wednesday morning, Minerva smilingly announced that the double wedding took place as scheduled.

"But how did you get a divorce so quickly?"

"Wellum," she said, "us all git tuh talkin' ' mong ouhrselves an' decided not tuh waste money fussin' 'roun' de cote-house. So, we jes' tuck dem sixteen dollahs an' bought a hangin' lamp!"

AN IMPERTINENT QUESTION

A young Negro woman appeared at the registration booth to procure a voting certificate.

"What is your name?" inquired the officer.

"Susannah Estelle Jenkins," came the answer.

"What party do you affiliate with?"

"Jedge, does Ah have tuh tell dat?" inquired the woman resentfully.

"Yes, it is required by law if you vote."

"Den, Ah jus' doesn't vote," said the maiden scornfully. "Jes' tear up dat wuthless vote an' stop meddlin' wid mah exaspera- tions. De party whut Ah 'filiates wid ain't eben got no divo'ce yit!"

The Evolution of Shakespeare

Old Aunt Liza was dusting the drawing room in a Southern home. She worked dili- gently until she came to a bronze bust of Shakespeare. She observed it cautiously, dusted a little, then hesitated.

"Miz Juliet, chile, who am dis good lookin' gemman heah?" she asked.

"That's Shakespeare, a great poet, who lived and died across the sea," answered the woman.

"Is dat him? Ah's done heerd lots ob Mistah Shakingspear fum de white folks an' de cullud folks, but bless my soul, Ah allers thought be'fo' dat he wuz er white gemman!"

Tobe:—"Didn't Ah see yo' kissin' a no- count piece o' trash las' night?"

Liza:—"It wuz dahrk an' Ah thought it wuz you."

Tobe:—"Come tuh think 'bout it, mebbe hit wuz me. Whut time wuz dat?"

COMMERCIALIZED GRACE

Mose Hampton, Negro proprietor of a barber shop for white people, was shaving one of his customers. The conversation dwelt upon the former connection of Mose with the African Church of the city.

"I believe you are still a member of this church, aren't you, Mose?"

"No suh, not dis yeah, Mistah Howard. Ah's done back-slid," answered the Negro.

"If I may ask, why did you leave the church after such faithful service?"

"Well, suh, hit wuz lak dis: When Ah jines de Chu'ch by babtism, Ah wuz 'thusiastically received by de brethren. In de fust yeah, Ah give'm ten dollahs, an' dey called me 'Bruddah Hampton'. De secon' yeah, bus'ness wuzent good, so Ah give'm jes' five dollahs. Den dey called me 'Mistah Hampton'. Well, de third yeah, Ah felt po're 'cause ob sickness, an' couldn't give'm nuthin.' Den dey called me 'dat ole Niggah Mose' an' said Ah wuz back-slidin'. Mistah Howard, dat's why Ah left 'em."

Rufus:—"How many yahrds do it take tuh make a shirt like dat?"

Rastus:—"Ah got two like dis out'n one yahrd last night."

MATTER AND SPACE

The local passenger train was very crowded. People were jammed in every nook and corner of the train. Especially was this true of the coach reserved by the Jim Crow laws for the exclusive use of Negro passengers.

Among the passengers of this coach was a colored woman of large frame and much corpulence. As the conductor pushed his way through the jam, his progress was arrested by some invisible object in the vicinity of the heroine just mentioned.

"Madam," said the conductor, "you must not leave your valise in the aisle of the coach. Please remove it at once."

"Fuh de lan' sakes, man," retorted the woman, "dat ain't no valise. Dat's mah foot, an' dey ain't no whar else tuh put hit!"

Judge:—"Are you sure he was home that night?"

Woman:—"Ef he wuzent, Ah suah busted a good rollin' pin ovah de haid ob a puffeckly innercent man!"

White Friend:—"Zeb, the Lord certainly smiled on you to give you two such fine children."

Zeb:—"Yassuh, but Ah's sho' glad he didn't laff out loud!"

A COURTEOUS ANSWER

The corpulent but polite Negro woman was doing much window shopping, but she was making no purchases.

Finally, she entered a store, and a clerk advanced to inquire if she wanted anything. To this, the huge brunette bowed her head politely and answered:

"Nossuh, Ah doesn't b'lieve Ah keers tuh refuse nuthin', please."

BEYOND HIS JURISDICTION

A party of New Yorkers were hunting in the "piney woods" of Georgia. They had as an attendant an old Negro who had a particular fondness for big words and whose originality gave genuine entertainment to the visitors.

One of the party, knowing the old Negro's bent, addressed him as follows:

"Uncle Mose, the indentations in terra firma in this locality render traveling in a vehicular conveyance without springs decidedly objectionable and automatically painful. Don't you think so?"

Uncle Mose scratched his left ear slowly, and with a pensive shake of his woolly head replied:

"Mistah Gawge, de exhuberance ob yo' verbosity am beyon' mah jurydiction!"

CPSIA information can be obtained at www.ICGtesting.com
Printed in the USA
LVOW011821291111

257009LV00026B/251/P